CORONATION
COMMENTARY

GEOFFREY DENNIS

—

CORONATION COMMENTARY

London
WILLIAM HEINEMANN LTD
1937

PRINTED IN GREAT BRITAIN
AT THE WINDMILL PRESS, KINGSWOOD, SURREY

CONTENTS

PUBLISHER'S NOTE

THE FOLLOWING BOOK, up to and including the chapter *Edward VIII*, was written during and 'in the spirit of' that monarch's reign. After reflection and consultation, the publisher with the author's agreement took the view that the balance of advantage lay with leaving the book exactly as written. No verbal change, however slight, has therefore been made by way of trying to fit the text to events that came after. In the publisher's view the curious prescience of those events which the text evinces is not the least argument for having left it alone.

The later portion of the book has been written since, and in the light of, the December happenings.

INTRODUCTION

MOST COUNTRIES ARE REPUBLICS. Our King is about the only serious king left.

Far away in the east there is, indeed, the mysterious Mikado, withdrawn from our western understanding as mainly from his own subjects' prostrate sight; the lineal descendant of the Son of Heaven, who twenty-five centuries ago came down to rule on earth; still more a god than a king. In one first-rank country of Europe, a shadow monarch still sits upon a shadowed throne. There are the three Scandinavian kings. There are the five Balkan kinglets. It would be injustice to the former, none however of whose kingdoms equals the population of London, and who have neither royal might nor imperial function, to class them as no more than glorified hereditary Lord Mayors; and to the latter, given the personal worth of two or three of them and the comparative stability of one or two of their thrones, to range them as mere operetta princelings, Ruritanian mummers on a scene that continually shifts. There is the Queen of Holland. There is the now model Belgian throne.

But, among the little lands as among the large, republics are the great majority.

It was not so until yesterday. When most of us

were born, and still when many of us were grown-up, there was Kaiser, and Austrian Kaiser, and Tsar, and Sultan: the four tremendous crowns the War sent flying. The Most Catholic Kingship vanished even more lately; the Dragon Throne not much earlier; the Kingdom of Portugal and her daughter Empire of the Brazils not much earlier again. Less than a generation ago, very nearly all the people living in the world, except Frenchmen and most inhabitants of the Americas, were subjects of emperors or kings.

The greatest country has withstood the current, and kept its king. The greatest in area and population, in dispersion and variety; the greatest, all points considered, in power and influence still. Of the world empires we, the chief one, alone conserve the emperor.

It is a matter for meditation; possibly for pride.

There are, no doubt, more momentous matters on which one might meditate.

Matters of life and death, and of Life and of Death. Religion: its present weakness and uncertain prospects; the age's ignorance of God, and rudderless course. Science: its spectacular successes and more spectacular failure; the effect of its guessings on our theoretical view of man in the universe; the results, good and evil, of its practical application by man in this world. The increasing complexity of human existence; man's stationary ability to cope with it;

the decreasing power of resistance to it of his nerves, and nerve. The threat of over-population, under-population—multiplication like mice, or race-suicide and the final vanishment of man? Reform of the economic and financial system: to make it work better, and to produce results less unjust and less absurd. Health and disease; education and ignorance; humanity and cruelty. To provide up-to-date government and efficient government and inspiring government while preserving fairly sane and fairly free government; while saving us from savagery, hysteria, hate. To save the beauty of England, what is left of it. To save us all from our tribal malady, war. To save civilization, if it may be saved, if it is worth saving. To save mankind, which has rejected the old salvation and found none other.

Compared with problems such as these, *Kings* may seem a trivial topic.

Yet you have a thousand books on science or economics to one on monarchy, thirty on the gold standard to one on the king's Golden Crown. The lesser topic—which has bearing too on some of the greater ones—may be worth its one book in the thirty or thousand. This is a humble such book.

THE
LAST
HUNDRED
YEARS

I

MONARCHICAL sentiment in England fell with the fall of the Stuarts.

The House of Brunswick had nothing but remote kinship to justify its kingship—some said fifty-seven persons had a better title than Elector George, others that there were only fifty-three. It had no claim to anyone's regard except, negatively, as being an insurance policy against something worse: against King James III, royal but Romish, in his train confessors and sly Jesuits, behind him the giant shadows of King Lewis and King Pope:

> *King George our Defender*
> *From Pope and Pretender.*

With the advent of these petty parliamentary princelings, not of the line legitimate—

> *Wha the deil hae we gotten for a King,*
> *But a wee wee German Lairdie?—*

there perished together the principle and the reverence upon which the ancient loyalty had been based.

Nor could men revere for himself this boorish Elector, with his dirty rapacious old mistresses; this foreigner whom they made lord over England, monstrously, though he could speak not one word of her language nor had the grace to try to; this dull, callous, un-royal man with his dingy Court, bare of all princeliness or pomp; this intruder who was interested in England only for what he could wring out of her. Sentiment, with loyalty, took wing Over the Water.

By the fact also that the title to it was in dispute, reverence for the Crown diminished. As a subject of political debate, its sanctity dwindled. The Whigs used it for their party ends, as a mere instrument of their power, according it as little respect as was feasible. The Tories, its natural champions, talked republican and 'made converts of themselves by their hypocrisy.'

For all the advantage which the German rule conferred, and not only upon the Whig lords and the City, the heart of the people never was with it— as late as 1777 Doctor Johnson believed that if England was fairly polled, she would vote Jacobite —and so monarchy was divorced from its true function, the representation of the whole nation. Under the first two Georges the kingly office counted for less, alike in the governance and imagination of England, than ever until that day.

With George the Third there was a change. He

gloried in the name of Briton. The throne won back somewhat, and for a while, of both power and esteem.

But even Farmer George, much the best liked of the five men who wore the crown of England between the brilliant reigns of the two women, heard cries when he rode abroad of "Remember Charles the First! Remember James the Second!"; saw the fists of the mob shaken in his face and their stones breaking through the glass of his coach as he moved, in solemn state, to open the Parliament. "Down with tyrants!" they shouted, "No King!"

> *Folks say it was lucky the stone missed the head,*
> *When lately at Cæsar 'twas thrown.*
> *I think very different from thousands indeed:—*
> *'Twas a lucky escape for the stone.*

Another time he was half dragged out of his carriage by ruffians, and rescued with difficulty by his guards. The upper classes, meanwhile, freely canvassed the abolition of the royal office.

It held out. The king after all was an Englishman; he would not so much as set foot in Hanover. He lived in decent domesticity; he liked boiled mutton and turnips.

He was brave and friendly. He was at least less unpopular than the politicians he was at loggerheads with: the Fox-North coalition, and others. He was

9   B

at least preferable to the Whig aristocrats who denounced him: while he was merely trying to get back some of their power (not the people's), they were living lives of heartless luxury and debauchery —and enclosing the common lands. He at least made no money out of power, as they did. Finally, the ferocious example of the Revolution across the Channel made men prefer the ills they knew of.

The French wars ended. The fear of the Revolution faded. Hatred gathered against the Crown, which all reformers regarded as the symbol and chief instrument of the harsh repressions of the long anti-Jacobin years. The old king went mad, and blind, alone high up in Windsor Tower singing snatches of Handel. The Royal Family of England was now his misliked brood of sons. Monarchy dived down steeply to its low point.

Between the traditional traducers of those Georgian brothers and their latter-day whitewashers the judgment of history, and of Heaven, may hesitate. What their country then thought of them was informed by no hesitation at all. Their country loathed them. For their sordid and quarrelsome lives; their vices, their venality; their debts which an impoverished overtaxed nation had to pay, and pay, and pay again; for their brutal reactionary politics. The Duke of Wellington, at one extreme, declared that the Royal Dukes had "insulted, personally insulted, two-thirds of the gentlemen of

England"; and that they were "the damndest mill-
stones about the neck of any Government that could
be imagined." To the common people, to moderate
decent men, to idealists like Godwin and Shelley,
they made it nightmare plain that royalty was
tyranny, oppression, beastliness:

> *Oh that the free would stamp the impious name*
> *Of King into the dust!*

Maybe the Prince of Wales had taste, and charm;
the Duke of York courage; the Dukes of Clarence
and Kent good nature; the Duke of Cumberland, the
horrible one-eyed Man with the Moustaches, ability.
In the eyes of the English people they were a crew of
thieves, bullies, scoundrels, sots and rakes.

Unfortunately, the one who first as Regent and
then King became the ruler of the country was
except for brother Cumberland the most unpopular
of the lot. Unlike the rest of the Hanoverians he was
a coward. To his people the First Gentleman in
Europe looked more like its last blackguard. On
his gross person he spent literal millions of the
country's money. He betrayed the liberalism he
had affected. He was fat, false, bestially selfish,
dissolute, drunken. He was hated savagely. The
best proof of his frightful unpopularity is that he
could confer a measure of popularity on so frightful
a person as his wife.

11

He was afraid of going out, for in the streets they hissed him; as he cowered back in his coach, the crowd clung to the wheels spitting and cursing. There were riots; an insurrection was feared in the North. If the mob savagely hated, the nascent middle class strongly disliked and the aristocracy despised him. At the Academy dinner, while the toast of the Duke of Wellington was given with enthusiasm, that of 'our magnificent patron'—His Majesty—was received in glacial silence.

When the spiteful bill he sponsored to deprive Caroline of her title of Queen had to be dropped, London illuminated. When she died, broken-hearted, a week or two after the Coronation from which he had succeeded in excluding her, London tore up trees and placed them across the road to prevent her dead body—her coffin blazoned "The Injured Queen of England"—taking the route, the shamefaced sneaking route, her lord had ordained.

Napoleon, reflecting at St. Helena on one change of dynasty lately accomplished, opined that England would soon change hers. Just before the Queen's death, the great Emperor died. A minister conveyed to the English king those tremendous tidings: "Your greatest enemy is dead, Sir." "Is she indeed, by God!" replied His Majesty.

For the miseries, and the materialism, of the epoch Florizel himself was not of course responsible: not for the child slavery in the factories, nor other

12

excesses of the Industrial Revolution then in its pitiless youth, nor the hunger, nor the harsh system of poor relief, nor the cruel laws, nor the enclosure of the people's land; nor even, except by brilliant example, for the dullness of mind and drunken ruffianism of society. A century of politicians, not kings, had produced that.

Despite even George the Fourth, the throne survived. With the upper class the ministers were almost as unpopular as the King himself; the poor, whether half-starving serfs in the counties or haggard slaves in the new factories in the towns, hated their near and seen oppressors much more than the irrelevant fat monster away in London. There was fear of the unknown, and always of the Revolution; reluctance to dispense with an institution as old as England itself, and substitute—what? The country still kept it, because of the complications of abolishing it; out of inertia, out of habit; out of hope. It was the very old title of the firm.

William the Fourth inspired less hatred than his brother—he was a friendly old fool, and doted on his ten illegitimate children—but not more respect. His half-daft speeches were the terror of his Ministry and the joke of the country, while behind him loomed the shape of the ogreish Duke of Cumberland, who might well become next king; whose accession, commented a member of the upper class, would be the moment for suppressing the post altogether. King Billy was jeered at in public; hooted and pelted as he came back from the play. Poverty, hunger and discontent stalked through the land. In France the expulsion of the last of the Bourbons set a new example, less forbidding than the first, of how to deal with kings.

The passing of the great Reform Bill of 1832 was, by its supporters and opponents alike, believed to be the first step in a general transformation of our institutions: the disestablishment of the Church, the disappearance of the House of Lords, and above all the abolition of the Monarchy. Old William doddered along ingloriously for a few years, and died in 1837; our last king who was a failure.

That hour was the lowest.

The reason, largely, was the character of the three successive kings who had worn the crown: a lunatic, a profligate cad and a buffoon. An obscure young girl ascended the ancient throne. In the one hundred years, exactly, since that hour the monarchy has risen from the depths to its present strange high place. The reason, chiefly, is the character of the three successive monarchs who came after.

II

How many prophets in 1837 would have foretold the existence of the British Monarchy in 1937?

To liberal minds of the earlier year, awake to the widening potentialities of material advance and moral advance, steam and education, human inventions and humane endeavour, Royalty—when they thought about it—seemed a tinsel trapping and anachronism that was bound before long to go. The last coronation Westminster will see, was the saying at Queen Victoria's.

She started, however, with a few things in her favour.

As when, in another age and land, the magnates had unsheathed their swords and cried to heaven *Moriamur pro rege nostro, Maria Theresa!*, so in industrial nineteenth-century England the idea of a girl as the head of the nation aroused romantic feeling. Chivalrous sentiment could gather itself about a Crown personified by a fresh young girl instead of selfish dirty old men; from whom, and from horrible Uncle Cumberland in particular, had she not saved the nation? She was a relief.

If there were some murmurings against a female, on balance the new sovereign's sex was an advantage. She was a novelty. Glorious Gloriana's and good Queen Anne's were the two reigns that stood out brightest in popular tradition. She was a hope.

And hope was in the air. Lord John Russell prayed that the young sovereign lady's reign might see crime and cruelty wane, education become more general, slavery abolished (it did, all three); and that it might become great and celebrated in history

15

(it has). The preachers in their pulpits and many of the people in their hearts, with a few of the newspapers, greeted her expectantly.

By the reform of the poor law and the penal laws and the break-up of the whole system of anti-Jacobin repression, the Crown, associated in men's minds with all these, stood to gain. Fortunately the Queen was just of age; so no need of a Regency—ill-sounding word—to complicate matters and perpetuate the rule of the ugly uncles. Jacobitism was dead. Henry the Ninth was; and even in Northumberland, even in North Wales, where the Cycle of the White Rose had faded into mere picturesqueness, even in the remotest Papist Highlands of Scotland, even in Manchester itself, loyalty to the old line was of the past.

What royalist sentiment there was gathered accordingly around this tiny German girl.

The dressing-gown scene in Kensington Palace, when they came to tell her she was Queen, was a pleasant curtain-raiser. Lord Melbourne at once sought to bring the young lady into high relief, and made the most of the convention that he was the minister not of Parliament but of the Queen. She shewed spirit. She frankly enjoyed her position, and many of her subjects frankly enjoyed her enjoyment of it.

She started with few other advantages.

Her office was disliked and mistrusted. The complicated series of deaths by which the throne had become hers threw into prominence the absurdity, the enormity, of the hereditary principle: who was she but the child of one of the obscurer of George the Third's sons, an old man that, most reluctantly, had given up his mistress and taken a wife on the part chance of producing a royal heir? Who was she herself but an exceedingly obscure young female whom obsolete principles and a series of accidents had elevated to the headship of the land? Plain Miss Guelph she had been born, and plain Miss Guelph it would have been better for all concerned had she remained.

She was a foreigner, anyway, of pure German stock renewed by a blatantly German mother; a mother who, with her paramour Sir John Conroy and other hangers-on—the Con-royal Family—was an unwanted meddler in the affairs of a country not her own. The daughter had only been born in England by the narrowest of squeaks, her father having driven her mother post-haste across the father and mother land of them all to achieve it.

Her name was foreign. There was something grotesquely un-English about 'Victoria.' Sir Walter Scott hoped she would have the sense to change it. In 1837 he could not foresee that—in 1937—Victoria would be the name of a great State, an important city, innumerable towns, villages, lakes, streets, parks, buildings: the most natural and widespread appellation in the British Empire.

She was a known partisan, bound to the Whigs and bitterly hostile to the Tories, who assailed her with venom; at True Blue dinners calumnious attacks on her were received with loud shouts of applause.

She was under five feet high. Not her most loyal subject could fancy her good-looking; not the most imaginative flatterer could imagine her distinguished or brilliant or anything but raw, goggle-eyed and commonplace.

She began badly.

Her conduct at her first Council, her royal bearing and facility, were indeed favourably commented upon by the few who witnessed them. But she put herself entirely in Lord Melbourne's hands and became a party Queen; she conducted herself as the personal enemy, not impartial sovereign, of Sir Robert Peel. There was the row over the Ladies of the Bed-chamber—wretched royal interference beginning all over again—and the row over Lady Flora Hastings. A certain shocking suggestion was made about that respectable Court dame. The young Virgin Queen (acting of course on the advice of Melbourne, who should have known better) gave orders that the elder female should be medically examined. From probing hands the Lady Flora emerged unscathed, and then the storm broke. The *Morning Post* commiserated with the slandered noblewoman as the "victim of a depraved court," and of its depraved young head in particular. "Her popularity has sunk to zero, and loyalty is a dead letter," noted Greville. At Ascot a duchess hissed her. *Mrs. Melbourne* jeered the crowd.

She married unpopularly. For husband must needs choose a German, an obscure German, a much too German German. In her partisan violence she refused to invite Tories, at first not even the national hero the Duke of Wellington, to her wedding. The Commons retorted by reducing the Consort's allowance. Her marriage was believed to increase, and did increase, her interest in German affairs. There was said to be, and perhaps there was, a conflict between family and national interests. She was suspected of loving the monarchy more than the country, and the man more than either. On the other side, some sentiment gathered in her favour for having broken royal rules and married a man she loved; and the rising middle class was soon able to admire her marital fidelity, so rare in recent monarchs, so like their own.

She started producing children. How German they would be, with such a mother, with such a father! Why had German Albert been put before English Edward among the baby Prince of Wales's names? The new humorous journal, *Punch*, made obscene jokes about her confinements.

Even her good points were counted against her.

She disliked war, and with her husband stood out against the jingoes, and Lord Palmerston their leader,

in the first enthusiasm for the useless Crimean War.
The Press covered the pacifist royal pair with every
sort of ridicule and abuse:

> Last Monday night, all in a fright,
>   Al. out of bed did tumble.
> The German lad was raving mad,
>   How he did groan and grumble!
> He cried to Vic, "I've cut my stick;
>   To Petersburg go right slap."
> When Vic, 'tis said, jumped out of bed,
>   And wopped him with her night-cap.

There was a howl when Palmerston resigned. "My
being committed to the Tower," wrote the Prince
Consort, "was believed all over the country, nay even
that the Queen had been arrested. People surrounded
the Tower in thousands to see us brought to it."

Though a stout Protestant, she disavowed religious
bigotry: the No-Popery passion of her uncles and the
middle classes and the mob. When, From without
the Flaminian Gate, the re-establishment of the
Roman hierarchy in England was pontifically
announced, she despised the hysterical fear which the
announcement inspired in her ministers. She could
never abide the fat worldly bishops of her Established
Church.

She frowned on race prejudice, and was reviled
by the Anglo-Indians for her insistence upon mercy
and moderation after the Mutiny.

She was for Free Trade and the repeal of the Corn Laws, which the bulk of the upper classes opposed.

Meantime the Radicals had no use for her. If the Six Points of the Chartists did not specifically include the abolition of the throne, in 1848, the year of European revolution, there was real fear of revolution in England also: the Cabinet proposed sending the royal children to Osborne for safety. The Queen herself was gloomy as to her future. A shower of rain sufficed to scatter the Chartist legions; and the sky cleared again.

In the eyes of the ardent various world of the forties and fifties, the world of industrial and scientific progress, and railways and rationalism and optimism, of Dickens and Stuart Mill, of splendid poetry, of Tractarian and Evangelical enthusiasm, she was a mere irrelevance. The aristocracy, still awhile Regency in modes and morals—the drinking, dicing, wenching, foul-mouthed men of quality—sneered at the purity, the prudishness, of her Court from which gay lords, and gay ladies, were rigidly excluded.

On this point they had indeed reason to be surprised as well as annoyed. Victoria and Albert were, by their ancestry, a queer couple to be models of sexual virtue. All four parents had been devotees of the flesh. The Duke of Kent with his mistresses; the Duchess with her gentleman friends. Albert's papa had had a blacksmith raise his hammer against him for undesired attentions to the blacksmith's very young daughter; Albert's frisky young mama had been divorced for adultery. The dear Uncle Leopold of both of them was a lady's man with a vengeance. Yet here was a court without mistresses or masters. Left to herself, the heady young Queen might perhaps have gone the way of her gay Georgian blood: it is an interesting reflection. But this alien mate, in prim reaction against the memories of his own early life, directed her differently; which, in the eyes of the libertine lords, was an unpatriotic redoubling of the offence.

The young foreigner's influence could be seen at work in the Court's championship of all the kings, while the country preferred their rightly rebellious subjects; in its opposition to the great Palmerston, insolent John Bull incarnate; in its aim, not quite wrongly believed to be Prince Albert's aim, of turning the machine of Cabinet government backwards, and having the sovereign again as permanent president of the ministry. From the Tories, from the Radicals, from many who were neither, throughout the fifties cries of hatred and mockery rose up continually against him.

Fortunately perhaps for the Monarchy, this unfortunate personage, who up to his last hour was working early and late for what he believed to be the good of his adopted country, whose last act was to soften a Palmerstonian draft to the American

Government, which in its crude original form might have meant war—which maybe Mr. Secretary Seward foolishly half-hoped might be crude enough to mean war—fortunately this intrusive personage soon died.

The Queen's unpopularity did not diminish. It grew.

In her extreme grief for the passionately loved husband—the long morbid mourning that followed that first wild shriek which had rung through the Castle when she *knew*—she withdrew into a fantastic privacy where the ceremonial function of the Crown was no longer exercised. This was bad for the dignity of the Constitution, bad for the shop-keepers and the sightseers and exceedingly unpopular everywhere.

She abandoned the capital and divided her life between the three secluded palaces of Windsor, Osborne and Balmoral, to the great inconvenience of the business of government and the growing dissatisfaction of her people, who hardly ever saw her, not one in a thousand of whom knew her by sight. She was blind to the need, for the very preservation of the monarchy, of a measure of visual popularity and concession in outward things.

In the sixties and seventies, the fifties of her own age, she was at her most unattractive personally, physically. She was no longer the enthusiastic girl,

23

nor the happy young married woman; while the venerable splendour of her old age lurked, unguessed at, still far away.

In foreign affairs her views, decided and perhaps at times decisive, became yet more unpopular. She objected to Garibaldi, whom England idolized. She favoured Prussia in the affair of the Duchies, and helped to prevent eager England going to war, a knight-errant on the side of Denmark.

As she by her too secluded life, so her young son and heir by his over-gay one was earning disapproval. The Prince of Wales was thought to be a mere rake and spendthrift. He was computed to attend thirty race-meetings a year. He cared only for the fastest society, male and other. At the time of the Mordaunt divorce case, both at Epsom and in a London theatre he was loudly hooted. Another George IV ahead.

Few thought he would ever reign; if Victoria had died ten years after the Prince Consort she might well have been our last monarch. In any case she would hardly have been remembered as a successful one.

It is well to die at the right moment. If John Keats had lived on earth as long as William Wordsworth, he might have lived in posterity as a dull old codger too. If Abraham Lincoln had not received the consecration of assassination before he had to face the problems of the after-war, he might never have become the American national saint and hero. If

24

the Kaiser had but died in 1913, he would have been William the Peacemaker.

Queen Victoria chose her hour wisely; and it was not in the difficult sixties and seventies.

Aside from the personal causes, the uprising in those years of anti-monarchy on the unfamiliar soil of England is capable of more general explanations.

The genius of two great historians had succeeded in changing, in the generation since Victoria's accession, the average Englishman's view of the story of his country. Before, the prevailing judgment on the great struggle between Crown and Cromwell had been favourable to the former and very unfavourable to the latter; by 1870 the opposite was the case. Thanks largely to Macaulay and Carlyle the educated classes, conservative and liberal alike, had become Whiggish in their seventeenth-century preferences and their nineteenth-century deductions. The national tradition of the Commonwealth as a time of anarchy and oppression and of the King as a fundamental necessity for England, which even the men of 1689 had deemed him, was—by literary talent, and the concording circumstances of an industrial and middle-class age—for a time almost completely overlaid. Thackeray's campaign against the Four Georges, displaying them in their most odious light, had reinforced the tendency against monarchy in general with renewed disrespect for the

25   c

House of Hanover in particular. That the eminent
romancer had launched his campaign in a foreign
country at £50 (or the dollar equivalent of £50) a
lecture, unpatriotically truckling to republican
snobbery, had indeed aroused criticism; but the
effect of *his* criticism, and of his facts, remained.

There were plenty of bad kings, grisly bad kings,
about in the Europe of that day to point the
republican moral. Gladstone had the conscience of
the country with him when he denounced atrocious
Bomba and the Neapolitan prisons. (Characteris-
tically, his enthusiasm for liberty in Southern Italy
was not coupled with enthusiasm for liberty in the
Southern States. In that country an ardent partisan
of the slavers, who were 'republicans', he had no
righteous wrath to spare from the dungeons of Naples
for the far more horrible flogging-dens of New
Orleans.) The enemies of the kings were heroes:
Garibaldi, Mazzini, Kossuth. Lincoln was a greater
man than any contemporary monarch.

The sensational fall of the greatest contemporary
monarch, Napoleon III, and the establishment of an
at last moderate republic in France, made an
enormous impression, despite English refractoriness
to foreign examples.

Mid-reign, that Whiggish hour that was the heyday
of Parliament, was for the monarchy an hour of
uncertain vocation. The old-fashioned type of
loyalty to it was moribund; its new national and

26

imperial career had not yet begun. The glamorous part of the Constitution was the Parliament. Pam, Dizzy and the blossoming Grand Old Man held the country's imagination. They were more interesting figures than the drab Widow of Windsor.

Sir Charles Dilke made his famous speech against the Queen at Newcastle. The principal Radical of the midlands, Joseph Chamberlain the rich mayor of Birmingham, came out in loud support of Dilke and announced the Republic "in our generation"; for the Prince of Wales's visit to the midland city, bets were laid against its mayor receiving him. Frederick Harrison declared the dawn of the English Republic to be "as certain as the rising of to-morrow's sun." John Bright and John Morley were of the same persuasion; and blind Fawcett, and blinder Green the historian. Swinburne was turning out republican odes. Herbert Spencer the philosopher, questioned about the Royal Family, replied philosophically: "I am not interested in the criminal classes."

The lower-middle-class section of the movement was led by Charles Bradlaugh; the Tribune, the Iconoclast. Republican clubs were founded throughout the country; chiefly by artisans in the industrial North but also in East Anglia, the old Ironside stronghold, and elsewhere.

On Sunday, September the 19th, 1870, a date now quite forgotten but which those present believed would be historic, at a tremendous meeting in

Trafalgar Square caps of liberty were hoisted on poles and they solemnly proclaimed the REPUBLIC OF ENGLAND.

Meantime the newspapers enjoyed themselves. The Queen's family was a "litter." The Prince of Wales was a "louse." He would never have the chance to "dishonour this country by becoming its King." His young child who prematurely died was a "rat," a "wretched abortion"; the parents' grief and the baby's funeral "sickening mummery at Sandringham." The Duke of Edinburgh was a common thief who had stolen from his ship's pay-chest. The Prince Consort's memory, dear to Her Germanic Majesty, was *dear* to her people also—had he not graciously left behind him a spawn of nine to be kept out of the taxpayers' pockets? And what—one need fall into no Brown study to guess the answer—what precisely were the functions of a certain stalwart Highland attendant upon Her Majesty's person?

This kind of thing was printed, read and spoken very widely.

While never sparing their scurrility, the Bradlaugh wing joined with Dilke and the rich men to spend their principal energies on Counting the Cost. The Queen was altogether too expensive. Was she *worth* £385,000 a year? Each one of the brood of nine was being provided for out of the public purse, yet still she came to Parliament "incessantly rattling the royal begging-box." She paid no income-tax. She made immense savings—Grandmother's Million—on her civil list, so as to provide fat dowries for her daughters and amass a private fortune. *What does she do with it?* was the pamphlet of the hour, while Charles in Trafalgar Square sneered at "princely paupers," and Sir Charles at Westminster moved a business-like motion enquiring how she spent her wage.

This appeal to self-interest and the middle-class ideal of economy was the part of the campaign that had most success. Certainly the proportion of the Budget that went on the throne—about one million pounds a year out of seventy millions—would seem high to-day. And certainly—the one point on which the Queen's enemies had the whole country with them—she was neither generously spending the money she got, nor giving value in return for it. She was paid to fulfil a great ceremonial function, and she did not fulfil that function. She was salaried as a mighty Queen and she lived, dingy and concealed, like a stingy private matron in a republic. The nation kept its side of the bargain. She did not keep hers. The nation said: We are getting too little monarchy for our money.

There lay the flaw in the whole argument. The discontent with the Queen was not because England wanted less monarchy, but because England wanted more.

All through this time, while the republican wave seemed to be gathering force, and towering, there had been a strong under-current the other way.

Now a personal happening in the Royal Family turned the tide sharply. The Prince of Wales fell dangerously ill. There was a movement of national sympathy, shewing what strength of feeling for the ancient Crown subsisted. The bulletin announcing the Prince out of danger was greeted with an outburst of genuine joy—the English *wanted* to like their Royal Family—and a violent reaction set in. The Queen's processional visit of thanksgiving to St. Paul's was the first of the monarchical ceremonies that marked the turn of the tide. Two days after the Thanksgiving Service an attempt on her life gave further force to the royalist wave.

Reynolds's Newspaper could sneer at "typhoid loyalty"; and John Richard Green, of whose Short History of the English People it has been not quite unfairly said that it is too short to mention the English people, could sourly comment that when Louis the Well-Beloved fell sick all France wept with anxiety, but '89 came never a year the later; and Dilke persevered awhile, and reopened his campaign against the Queen in Parliament. But only two honourable members voted for his motion and Bradlaugh, with more horse-sense than the others, confessed that the princely illness had "put the clock back fifty years." The republican clubs passed a tactful resolution of sympathy with Her Majesty, which "while not concealing our decided preference for a republic over a monarchical form of government," yet gave expression to "our desire, as Englishmen, to record our sorrow . . . our heartfelt sympathy . . . our sincere hope. . . ." Oddly English 'republican' clubs. In that strange resolution no click of the guillotine or clatter of the tumbrils, not in palest echo.

The Queen woke up. She seized the golden opportunity and under the impulsion of Dizzy's dazzling flattery and the Prince of Wales's sound advice began to come forth and fulfil again, at first rather grudgingly, the ceremonial obligations of her station. She rode in procession, visited hospitals, reviewed troops.

It became known that her seclusion had been partly due to ill-health. It came to be seen that the Prince was something more than a mere waster. His Princess, Alexandra of Denmark, was gracious and lovable. She helped the Prince to win a fair share of the new royal popularity. (If a quite miserable share, maintained Her Majesty, compared to Her Majesty's own:—"Everyone said that the difference shewn when *I* appeared, and when Bertie and Alix drive, was *not* to be described. Naturally for *them* no one stops, or *runs,* as they always did, and *do* doubly now, for *me*.")

The French Republic was not doing so well. The brand-new Spanish Republic, to which Bradlaugh as possible first Head of the English one had gone in pomp to convey fraternal greetings, was doing extremely badly.

So was the English one. Quickly, rather miserably, the famous agitation faded away and died. The leaders deserted, or took cover. The clubs disbanded. By the '80's the monarchy was stronger than for generations. Well before then, republican meetings could only be held under police protection.

If, through these difficult years, many—really rather unimportant—public men had been foes of the throne, the two men in England who mattered were its unflinching champions: Disraeli and Gladstone, the leaders of the two great parties, the leaders of England acknowledged as such in a way no later political men have distantly approached. The former it was who now led the Crown towards a new destiny as Symbol of Empire; the latter—who, if he had chosen to proclaim one half of what he suffered from the Queen, could still perhaps have made her position in the country as awkward as his with her— chose instead in his almost mediæval monarchical devotion to keep loyal silence.

The character of the champions of the republic did much to discredit them; and it. The ringleader,

> *Charlie Dilke*
> *Who spilt the milk*
> *Coming home from Chelsea,*

recanted to gain office, while his horrible private amusements hardly seemed to fit his self-appointed part of apostle of purer government, or of pure anything at all. His role, as the son of a courtier whom the Prince Consort had specially favoured, was strongly resented by the country and by the Queen.

> *What matter? Something whispers, 'Tis the*
> *mission of my life*
> *To spit my noxious venom on my*
> *benefactor's wife.*

When Victoria read his Newcastle attack upon herself she remarked that she remembered meeting him, as a boy, at the Great Exhibition. She remembered that she had stroked his hair. "I suppose," she added, "I stroked it the wrong way."

The quality of Dilke and Bradlaugh corresponded to the quality of the whole movement. It had been vicious; and it had been cheap and vulgar. Their pounds, shillings and pence argument seemed rather a poor argument on which to found a more idealist polity.

The anti-monarchy leaders had nothing to offer the working classes. Chamberlain, Cowan, Bright were rich manufacturers; the last, Bradlaugh's rival candidate for the Presidency of England, a classical capitalist of the Manchester School who at once smugly and savagely opposed factory reform and humaner conditions in the mills. Bradlaugh poked fun at Jesus Christ as at the Queen, impartially; but he held private property and masters' rights sacred.

As to the decent middle classes, they had by now become the ruling caste; and they saw the Queen as theirs. She had so many of the same virtues, and stood so largely for the same ideas. They learnt with quickening heart how, through the unpopular days of her retirement, she had worked conscientiously, early and late, at the business of the country; how she travelled to Balmoral or Osborne with literally hundreds of boxes filled with State documents that required her attention or her sign manual; how she would sign three hundred papers at a sitting, and read, write and sign later into the night than any clerk in her realm.

They rejoiced in the purity of her Court. The old mistress-flaunting bucks of Regency stripe were by this time elbowed out and the English poor, with their often parallel notions of amorous freedom, had not yet elbowed their way up. Rigid morality which in one short earlier period, the English Republic, had held the field, now for this second period, the renascence of the monarchy, held it again. The Queen loved her nine children, and had hoped for more—deplored that she had not had triplets. She loved no lover. No rakes or divorcees might enter her Court. No bankrupts; and she paid her debts.

How far her personal life was an example to, how far a fortunate coincidence with, the code of the dominant class, is not easy to determine; but the chance, lucky chance, that Victoria had bourgeois tastes and virtues in a period when these were uppermost, was the chief single fact among others contributing to her gradual popularity and the throne's continuance.

They rejoiced in her defects. She was a Philistine; she had no use for good painting, good music or good books. She opposed the claim, although she herself was the supreme and outrageous justification of it, to 'women's rights.' Lady C——, who advocated these, ought, said Her Majesty, 'to have a good whipping.' She disliked cleverness, as most of her subjects did. She disliked the Irish, as most of her English and Scottish subjects did.

This dislike and its consequences, her bleak refusal to be gracious to Ireland, may have had justification in her own mind: had not the Fenians tried to blow up a statue of the Prince Consort? It was the most tragic error of her reign. When Gladstone urged her to have a royal residence on the other side, she refused. When Disraeli reminded her that, in two hundred years, her predecessors had passed twenty-one *days* in the sister island, she sulked. When pressed by them both to spend at least more time there—in her own reign she passed seven years in Scotland, and not as many weeks in Ireland—she got angry. "It would be wasting time," she said, "when Scotland and England" (note the order) "*deserve* it so much more." Her Scottish and English subjects must take their share of the blame. They agreed with her heartily. Her dislike of Ireland was never a factor in her unpopularity.

Individual acts of hers appealed to the common imagination: her letter of condolence to Mrs. Lincoln, from a Widow to a Widow; her institution of the Victoria Cross, and improvement of its motto; her protest against the match tax, which she forced the Government to drop.

It was believed that, despite disagreement with some of her ministers, she had never gone beyond the Constitution, however strong her feelings. If Palmerston talked, Gladstone that misused monarchist did not. In his self-denying royalism, he continued heroically to defend her always, and further damped down the republican feeling in the Liberal Party. He, the old Radical, saved the throne.

It came to be seen that she had been as often right as wrong, and perhaps oftener right than her ministers, in the handling of foreign affairs. She had sought to prevent the senseless Crimean adventure, had prevented the war for the Danish Duchies, had moderated Prussia in the hour of victory in 1870, intervened strongly to prevent the new Imperial Germany from falling upon France a second time, made a stand against our 'drifting into war' in the Russo-Turkish conflict of 1877.

Meantime, by the eighties, the middle classes were less concerned about fighting for their rights against aristocracy and privilege—that fight they had won—than in fighting to defend their rights against the working classes and the poor.

For almost the whole of the rest of her reign, the politics of the country matched the Queen's. The Liberals were out. The Tories were in.

Imperialism arose, and the Queen became its glorious figure-head. The symbolism of Empire, Disraeli aiding, was from the outset identified with the symbolism of the Crown. The Queen herself had personally encouraged the new awareness of Empire; as when, years earlier, she had sent the boy Prince of Wales to tour Canada and so draw closer those ties which some of her servants in the Colonial office—and a younger Disraeli—thought on the contrary "might better be slackened." She gloried in the magnificent role of Empress of India, magnificent title she conferred upon herself in the teeth of the Cabinet and of Disraeli himself, who had made the suggestion as a kind of flattering joke. Over Gordon, popular passion was with her; and against her enemy, that cold-hearted villain Mr. Gladstone. Later, to her Diamond Jubilee, her apotheosis, she invited representatives of every part and race of the Empire, of the armed forces of the Empire, and

Princes of India, and Dyaks from Borneo, and Cypriotes and Chinese from Hong-Kong; and by all men the Crown that day was seen to be the chief link between them all.

Seclusion, a seclusion now known to be devoted wholly to affairs of State, ceased to be a reproach, and added mystery. She was the hidden idol of England.

Above all she was *old*. That is a distinction which it takes time to acquire; which could confer affection even on Mr. Gladstone and in our own day has made so improbable a figure as Mr. Bernard Shaw a hero of the classes he has spent his long life making fun of. Old age, glorified by the gathering legend of duty and devotion, and magnified by the people's belief that she was immortal, made her something more than monarch: made her matriarch, monument, myth.

She was a high and immovable part of Nature. She was like the Sun and the Moon.

Golden Jubilee, the fiftieth anniversary of her accession, England held as a national festival, the first of that series of public rejoicings which landmarks in the life of the Royal Family have ever since, with augmenting width and warmth, triumphantly become. The cape of kingly depression was turned for good.

Queen's weather again, and at Diamond Jubilee, by when her reign was the longest in our history and men thought it unending, they saw this tiny fat old woman, this plain honest old woman, as the emblem of English might, English virtue and English sovereignty over one-fifth of the people of the world. The Crown of this realm is a Crown Imperial, Henry the Eighth had said long ago. His diminutive successor had made it true.

Primitive peoples held her in awe—she was the Great White Queen—the nations of Europe in deepest respect. In the nineteenth century one hundred kings had ascended thrones in Europe, and now, the mightiest of them all, she was majestically entering the twentieth. Her own belief in herself was beyond ordinary human pride. She was the Anointed of the Lord. She and the country were one same thing; chimerically, divinely, matter-of-factly, she felt herself to be the centre, pivot, essence of the nation. And the nation felt it. She *belonged* to them. She was Number One in Country Number One. She knew it; and the country knew it. They rejoiced together in mutual affection and mutual pride.

Her power over the Jubilee crowds is said to have been magnetic, hypnotic. When the ride was over and the carriage entered the Palace gates, 'tears of pure thankfulness' gushed from her eyes; at the sight of which an emotion of frantic loyalty and answering tears seized all the people.

The few whisperings against her, still in these triumph days ventured, had small audience and short shrift. It was said that she did not shew much interest in social reforms: well, nor did her governments. That she was highly partisan: it was not believed, or was believed and gloried in. What little royal unpopularity was still available spent itself upon the Prince of Wales. During the Tranby Croft baccarat scandal, a journalist declared that the Prince's conduct was really not an adequate return for the 880,000,000 prayers which (the journalist calculated) England had offered up for him since his birth; and *Ich deal* was suggested as a new motto for his crest. No speck of this belated mud splashed the garments of Her Majesty his noble mother.

There was war in her ultimate hour; but she, whoever else had, could have no doubts of the African issue. She cut short the precautionary Mr. Balfour: "The possibilities of defeat do not interest us. *They do not exist.*" Her drives through the capital during the darkest war days, the closing days of her own life, aroused an enthusiasm excelling even Jubilee.

When, after a short illness during which millions of men and women throughout the British Empire had been praying for her, what everyone expected, what no-one could conceive of, in the course of Nature at long last took place, the miracle had been accomplished. The ancient institution so despised and so reviled when sixty-four years earlier she had begun to personify it now seemed to almost all

Englishmen the inevitable form of the headship of their State, and the glamorous sign and symbol of their national pride and unmatched imperial destiny.

III

The Queen is dead. Long live the *King!*

How odd the word sounded. There was something wrong about it; there was something not only unfamiliar but something unsuitable, something almost improper in having a *man* as the royal symbol. (Those were not our nine-year-old adjectives; but so, in the undoubted company of many other of his new Majesty's subjects, young and old, in January 1901 we intimately felt.) Monarchy was a feminine, an idealistic thing. One knew how men were made, physically. A king was all wrong.

To no tongue the strange word came readily. When we stood up in our little Dissenting chapel to sing the National Anthem, three-fourths of the congregation sang 'save the *Queen*' and 'Send *her* victorious' by mistake; or not by mistake.

In a world wider than ours the new ruler was felt curiously as anti-climax. With the Queen, not so much a woman as an everlasting landmark had gone; a century, an age of the world. The accession passed automatically; no single person spoke or thought the word Republic, so dead was the formidable agitation of but thirty years before, so high had the dead matriarch brought the Crown. But what, in comparison, could this amiable man of pleasure do? Sixty years an Heir Apparent. What, coming after Her, could he *be*? He won't be the King his mother was, said an Irishman.

Too fond of abroad, said the ordinary stay-at-home Englishman. Always gadding about with foreigners. Spoke English with a thick German accent, like George the Second. Then it had been "I don't like *b*oetry and I don't like *b*ainting"; now it was "I don't know much about *a*rrt, but I do know something about *a*rrrangement." In each case the sentiment was unexceptionable, but not the pronunciation.

Too fond of *Paris*, added the Nonconformists meaningly—there was Tranby Croft too, and he had won that wicked Derby—and with the luxurious imagination of Puritanism they envisaged their new sovereign lord, a huge cigar in his mouth and a white top-hat on his head, against a lurid Satanic background of race-courses, gaming tables, green-rooms, red lights, Frenchwomen and godless Smart Society. In our house it was sadly summed up, for juvenile ears modestly, by 'He plays cards' and 'He is not a teetotaller.'

Little indeed had God done in answer to his lamented Mother's fervent prayer that the son would grow up 'to resemble his father in *every, every* respect.' Little indeed had he himself done to fulfil

42

the programme of life laid down for him, long ago,
by that blameless sire:—'under the influence of per-
severing example, to devote his leisure time to the
fine arts, looking over drawings, engravings, etc.';
to eschew frivolity, smoking, all pleasures; to think
only of 'tasks'; to live a life in which the reading of
Sir Walter Scott should be deemed too light an
occupation, though the writing of summaries of
Gibbon's Decline and Fall of the Roman Empire
might, as riotous recreation, occasionally be allowed.
We were loyal, the most dissenting and Radical of
us—which shows where republicanism stood by
1901—but a *good* man our new king, alas, was not.

Ordinary people, while admitting that he was
probably better than painted, doubted if he could
become, whether a good man or not, a good *king*.

The Times—this was sign of the times—instead of
blackguarding the new sovereign, as a reign or two
earlier it would have done, patronized him merely.
"We shall not pretend," sniffed the Thunderer smugly,
"that there is nothing in his long career which those
who respect and admire him could wish otherwise."

That in fact the faults of this maligned personage
were of a minor order (he was peppery, testy,
touchy; a bit of a guzzler; of the earth rather earthy);
that he was a courteous and charming gentleman,
benign and friendly; had a large fund of information
and of tact, a keener sense of humour than most
kings, and a remarkable memory; was a shrewd, just,

43

liberal-minded, common-sense man of the world, certainly up to the average in ability and industry—all this was known, at the outset, to but a privileged few.

In the King's favour there told the excitements of a new reign, and of ceremonies that none but the aged had seen. On some minds the strange male word worked favourably. Queen meant Queen Victoria only; King revived memories of our ancient monarchical past and evoked, beyond the flat and forgotten Georges, high visions of state and glory long neglected but now, maybe, to be revived.

Yet even those most hopeful for him could not but see that a notable part of the awe, and sanctity, and mystery, of his office had departed from it with his mighty mother into the tomb.

At her going, there had been a queer first instant of hesitation, bewilderment; almost of fear. The end of that cosmic existence was hard to grasp. A new way of thinking had to be found, a new image somehow fashioned of a world without Queen Victoria. The giant legend dwarfing him, the best to hope for was that the King's different personality would permit the gradual development of a new type of loyalty and royal prestige.

He had a hard job ahead.

He began it well.

His short accession speech, spontaneous, prepared by no clerks, was judged admirable.

44

For his title, he at once set all our doubts at rest. "It would be *impossible* for you to *drop* your Father's name, it would be *monstrous;* yet *Albert* alone would *not do,* as there can only be *one Albert*." Disobeying the mandate of the imperious dead; declining the double name enjoined upon him, and the unpopular Albert altogether; declaring, with what mixture of sincerity and irony must be surmised, "That name shall stand alone" he chose merely to be Edward the Seventh: a name that was pleasing to all, and a number that was delightful to many.

He opened Parliament in person, which the Queen had not done for many years. In magnificent State Procession, with his gracious Consort beside him.

When they saw him and his beautiful queen, the first beautiful queen for centuries, in the light of the twentieth century riding gorgeously past with crowns, real great golden crowns, upon their heads; men and women and children were elated: the thrill was exquisite.

Supposed to be up to his ears in debts, it was learnt that he came to the throne without any. (It was not learnt who had paid them, or in return for what.)

He humorously shewed that he felt strong enough, against the legitimists at least, to place finger-bowls for the first time upon the royal dinner table.

Above all, once again he had the good fortune to fall dangerously ill.

That postponed Coronation was worth four. If sanctimonious, the English are generous. As the new king lay in mortal danger, and as slowly he recovered from it, they said: Let us give him a chance.

He deserved it.

First, he combined, as the Queen had not, a life of hard work at the political and documentary side of his job with frequent and majestic public appearance —which he enjoyed, as she had not—performing with splendour and a perfect royal dignity the full cere-monial duties of Majesty which had for forgotten generations fallen into abeyance. His enjoyment of pomp and public display communicated itself to his people. Buckingham Palace dusted and polished; parties and receptions given there; foreign monarchs gorgeously invited there. Courts at Edinburgh and Dublin. Chapters of the Garter convened, and the King of England leading the fantastic procession of the Knights to St. George's Chapel . . .

He made himself the brilliant head not only of a brilliant and amusing Court, the first Court in England since Charles the Second's that had not been boorish or boring, but of a whole nation in spectacular mood, audibly rejoicing in a Visible Head.

Times and men had changed. The monarch, this opulent magnificent monarch, was a more interesting person now than his ministers. Balfour and Campbell-Bannerman were not Gladstone or Disraeli, great figures who could keep the country's fascinated attention on Parliament, a rival interest to the Crown.

He enjoyed receiving deputations. Deputations enjoyed being received by him. Tongue-tied deliverers of addresses of welcome he would coach in a "fat cosy whisper."

What was known of his developing political activity was approved. Aware, better than his insular and jingo ministers, of the harm it was doing England everywhere and determined to stop it before his Coronation, he put an end to the unpopular South African War, personally forcing the acceptance of more generous terms for the Boers.

He visited Ireland and shewed and said that he liked the Irish. That people, never made for republicans, gave him warm liking in return. It was probably too late.

His foreign political journeys were approved of; if the importance of them, the wisdom of them—if his own ability as a diplomatist—was exaggerated by some. England was proud of a king who seemed to have such power in the counsels, such prestige in the eyes of the foreigner. As he had made Buckingham Palace, renovated, the social centre of London, so he made London in place of kingless Paris the social centre of the world; which ministered to the national pride, and to pride in him as author of the auspicious change. His liking for France and dislike of the Kaiser fitted, if it scarcely shaped, his subjects' new international likes and dislikes, forced upon them by new facts.

In home affairs he proved himself able and, unlike his mother and all remembered predecessors, wholly impartial. Mr. Balfour, from the heights of a philosophic mind and the impregnable fortress of a frosty heart, might possibly despise this matter-of-fact, popularity-loving, pomp-and-parade-loving man of the world with whom as his Master he had —well, well !—to reckon; the country as a whole soon formed a high judgment of his personality and capacity. Seeing that the country took him seriously, he took himself more seriously. Within three years all the doubts at his accession were silenced; indeed forgotten.

When after the 1906 election the triumphant Liberals came in, a bit shy of kings, they were made very welcome. To their surprise and radical pleasure, Majesty preferred them to their predecessors. Their predecessors had been Lord Salisbury, slyly unsentimental about the Crown; Lord Lansdowne, a High Whig suspicious of kingly meddling; and Mr. Balfour. C.-B.— forthright, pawkily humorous, lover of France—was more His Majesty's idea of a Prime Minister, or at least of a man, than A.J.B., contemptuous, tortuous and detached. Haldane was much more his idea of a War Minister than Arnold-Forster. Throughout his long princehood a large proportion of his private friends had been Liberals.

48

These fortunate personal reasons balanced any political leaning the Crown might still, possibly, have had to the other side; Edward placed it absolutely outside and above the parties, and thus made his greatest contribution to its continuance.

Admirably filling his new self-appointed role of giver of advice to His Majesty's advisers, he fulfilled, without any lapse, the older constitutional part of following theirs; however distasteful, especially at the beginning with the Boer War jingoes and at the end with the Limehouse ranters, to him as a private person that advice might sometimes be. Politically he worked quite hard.

He had a good time also; kept up his round of visits to race meetings and country houses, entertained royally at Sandringham, went about everywhere with a gay band of amusing friends. Edwardian England liked to see him having it. Puritanism was on the down grade; whether or no the change was merely a fortunate coincidence for him, whether in some measure he contributed towards it. 1905 certainly minded less that he liked good food, pretty women, a race meeting, a flutter at cards, than 1875 would have minded. If more popular with the upper and the lower—"Good old Teddie!" they cried as he led in Minoru, first King to lead in a Derby winner —than with some sections of the middle classes, he won these over too. I remember the oddly different tone of Nonconformist talk in 1901 and 1910.

Genial and jovial, with the crowd he was the most popular king since Charles the Second. He was the Average Sensual Man *in excelsis*, and the sensual average man revelled in his own reflection in so majestic a mirror.

He made mistakes of course.

After Campbell-Bannerman's resignation he should never have summoned Asquith to Biarritz: abroad. He even mooted holding a Privy Council in Paris. Asquith said firmly No. It looked, to some, as though the royal comfort and convenience were being allowed to count for more than the interests and ancient traditions of the realm. There was sharp criticism, perhaps rather out of proportion to the crime committed.

He was too much on the Continent altogether. Was not Harrogate (asked we of that town, loyal to both him and it) as good a spa, with quite as great a variety of treatments, as all those outlandish Homburgs and Carlsbads and Marienbads? Why Biarritz—when there was Blackpool?

He could, with imperial advantage, have found time to visit one of the dominions. Canada twice sent him a pressing invitation; his reason for refusal, that in the difficult state of European affairs he did not want to be so far away from London, may have been adequate.

The first to accede as King of the United Kingdom

of Great Britain and Ireland and *the British Dominions beyond the Seas,* he altogether shewed rather scant interest in empire matters. He it was however who, after helping to stop the Boer War, had done much to reconcile the beaten foe by receiving Botha, de Wet, and Delarey privately on his yacht; and who, despite his Government's reluctance, accepted the offer of the Cullinan diamond. Refusal, he said, would have been a fatal 'bad snub' to the lately reconciled Transvaal Dutch who had generously made the offer.

He was unwise to exclude the Three Members— Mr. Keir Hardie, Mr. Victor Grayson, Mr. Arthur Ponsonby—from his garden party at Buckingham Palace, because they had protested in Parliament against his visit to Russia. He fancied some features of the Tsar's home policy no more than they did, but was doing his duty; as they no doubt theirs. The right of freedom of speech in the Commons was involved, and in the end he made amends with good grace. (He had wisely ignored the more virulent Mr. Ramsay Macdonald who, himself the greatest hobnobber of the age, accused him in the country of "hobnobbing with a bloodstained creature like the Tsar.")

He was in error, possibly, in letting it be known rather widely that Mr. Lloyd George was not his favourite minister nor Woman's Suffrage a cause he keenly cared for. But he treated the former with constitutional correctness, and the latter was no part of his Cabinet's policy. His Prime Minister disliked the Cause almost more than, and his colleague almost as much as, the King himself did. When he called the Welshman's limehousing 'Billingsgate,' the latter accepted the reproof gaily; and continued.

Unemployment was growing. Amid the misery of so many of his people, Edward looked too fond of luxury. He went around too much with the fast racing set, the very rich sets, and a collection of plutocratic Germans, Americans and Jews. The old gossip about the Prince Consort was occasionally revived: might he himself not be one of the Chosen People?

With his prestige, Edward might have acted as a barrier against the new tide of wealth and display, alien and native. Instead he let it flood.

On the other hand, he had some understanding of, and interest in, social questions; favouring not merely General Booth but remedial legislation also. He broke down stiffness, false gentility and our inhospitality to foreigners. When he went sailing with his friend Sir Thomas Lipton, others than snobs might regret that it was with a very rich grocer, or with Sir Thomas Lipton; only snobs that it was with a grocer.

It is a modest list really, this list of Seventh Edward's 'mistakes.' Cabinet ministers, presidents, dictators, Kaisers, might envy it.

The credit side was longer. Through years of

social change and tension, of drastic political change-over and at the end (Budget: Peers) high political excitement, he had—by his humane and genial personality, by political impartiality and ceremonial revival, by being both a mainspring and the brilliant figure-head of his time—made the nation's point of union yet more stable, and without democratic pose had further strengthened, popularized and illustrified the ancient Crown.

He kept peace in Europe in his day.

He died unexpectedly, when the nation still expected a twenty years' reign.

IV

Again the same curious moment of misgiving.

In his short reign of nine years Edward, like Victoria, had made himself an institution. Again it was, in part, the dead monarch's fault—the fault of a clear personality, rather than of gifts and achieve-ments which over the open grave Press and people were engaged in loudly and loyally exaggerating—that the heir started off with a handicap. It was, in part, the new monarch's own personality or, rather, presumed lack of it. George was unknown, untried. He was thought to be less adroit, less individual than his father, without his flair for Europe and for men; to have none of the shrewdness and tremendous will-power of his grandmother. His appearance was not very familiar, nor specially attractive to, his subjects; a beard, and an absurd resemblance to the Russian Tsar—that was all we saw. The Press didn't fancy him; he wasn't exciting copy. Doubt was general. At dinner on accession night Winston Churchill said: "Let us drink to the health of the new King." "No," replied Lord Crewe, "rather to the memory of the old one."

The feeling seems to have been more negative than definitely unfavourable. Keir Hardie stood almost alone in thinking that 'born in the ranks of the working class, the new king's most likely fate would have been that of a street-corner loafer.'

He was known to be sincere, unaffected and honourable. He had been a sailor, the best beloved of the professions; a real practical sailor, who had worked at his job. In command of a torpedo boat as a young man of twenty-four he had ably, and very gallantly, in a great gale off the Irish coast rescued another torpedo boat from a dangerous position. His courage was evident: it was courageous to call yourself George the Fifth.

He was said to be a country gentleman of the best type, with a model estate with model conditions of employment upon it, and among the finest breeds of cattle in the world. He liked clean sports, such as yachting and angling. The newspapers mentioned him, impressively, as the *second-best* shot in England.

He was at least—at last—an Englishman. He had no trace of German accent. In the eighth generation from Elector George that guttural noise at last was stilled.

This was all very pleasant. But qualities of kingship?

One qualification the croakers had to allow him: he knew the wide Empire over which he was called to rule as no earlier king had done, as not the most travelled of the Roman Emperors, not Trajan, had known the Empire of Rome. His young-manhood's cruises on the Bacchante had been comprehensive; his colonial tour at the beginning of his father's reign, when he had opened the first parliament of the Australian Commonwealth, had been a success beyond expectation and the run of royal progresses, had indeed positively *done* something to 'cement the Empire.' For the first time all the Dominions had seen the heir to their common Crown; the emotion aroused, political and personal, had been considerable and even lasting.

In this imperial spirit the new king began. He gave up his father's habit of visits to the Continent —he disliked the place as much as his father had liked it; the old marquess's motto 'I hate abroad,' could well have been his—and sailed east instead to announce himself Emperor to his three hundred million Indian lieges. The Delhi Durbar of 1911 is reckoned among the gorgeous ceremonies of history;

while the declaration of benefits the King-Emperor read out, when Viceroy and Princes had done him homage, was a more practical one than has sometimes accompanied such festivals, not forgetting the most humble classes of the sub-continent, nor the poorest.

The tone of the Court changed. The foreigners and the racing crowd and the men and women of pleasure were shewn the door. This was popular with the middle class and was taken in good part by nearly everybody, except those directly touched; so monarchically eager were the English to find good points in their sovereign, even at the expense of implied criticism (to which they shut their illogical eyes) of the sovereign who had gone before.

Of some aspects of the late reign it is not yet possible to speak with certainty, or propriety. Of the exact part George played as a constitutional king not much is known, except that it was constitutional. Both in the 'Peers-People' clash which noisily greeted his accession and in the Home Rule crisis of just before the War he intervened on both sides for moderation. In neither the Curragh Camp affair nor the formation of the National Government in 1931 is there any evidence that His late Majesty played other than a carefully correct part.

Some of the robuster Radicals had their suspicions, however. When they heard, or imagined, a report that George had point-blank refused to create the peers to pass the Parliament Bill there was, pretty well for the last time, a flare-up of anti-king talk. Hotheads at the National Liberal Club, fancying themselves back in the eighteen-seventies, thought of holding a republican demonstration in Trafalgar Square, and proposed fighting the new election on 'The King and the Peers versus the People.' They thought better of it; they calmed down. The report was false.

The King never once, not under the severest temptation of unjust accusation, expressed his own private views on Home Rule or the Lords. He absolutely refused to take sides. For this some of the hotter Tories in their turn assailed him. It was the King's business to take sides—with them.

From whichever side, or from neither, out came the Malta Marriage lie, and the intemperance lie. These were resented by almost everybody.

For King George had already begun to acquire, by his modesty and devotion to duty, a good measure of general esteem. It was never his father's easy popularity. In the rather improbable event of his having won the Derby, it is yet more improbable that the crowd would have slapped him on the back and called him 'Good old Georgie!'

In the War he obeyed his sense of duty; and politically his ministers. He did what they and the national situation and the civilian nature of his kingship required. He reviewed troops leaving for

France, visited the Grand Fleet and the Western Front, inspected hospitals, ambulances, munition factories. Dull work; fairly useful work. Respect for the King and his quiet decency was a valuable, though not decisive, sentiment of those violent days.

Towards the end of the War were heard the feeble final splutterings of anti-monarchy. The Royal Family was whispered to have encouraged, or at least allowed, its kinsman Tino King of Greece to stand up to the Allies; to be intriguing against the new republican Russia. Cries against the King were said to have been raised in certain regiments. Soldiers—Australians in one version of the story—in theatres were said to refuse to stand up for the National Anthem. The Irish element in the big cities was often disloyal: from our point of view, not theirs. While others bled and died, royalty stayed safe in its palaces. They were Germans. They were Boches. They were Huns. The Hidden Hand . . .

This talk died away as quickly as it had arisen. The House of Windsor was proclaimed; the Kaiser did the one witty thing recorded of him, and desired a command performance of the Merry Wives of Saxe-Coburg-Gotha; and Armistice Night saw the Palace the centre of the national joy and emotion.

The post-War years were a period of effacement. In the world as a whole monarchy, which the belief

and the propaganda of the moment made responsible
for the War, had collapsed in catastrophe; and stood
at its lowest place in history. Tsar, Austrian
Emperor, Sultan, Kaiser, all were gone, and none in
glory. Three unmonarchical men, Wilson, Lloyd
George and Clemenceau, had won the greatest war
of time and were promising the greatest and most
profitable peace. Kingship had failed. It was an old
thing done with. Every single one of the new
countries the Peace set up became a republic. In
England, while nobody sought or desired a change,
the throne seemed irrelevant to the excitements,
difficulties and central hopes of the day. It was simply
not thought about. King George was out of the
picture: Lloyd George was in it. Whether or no it
was that the tribune deliberately depressed the king's
role or that two such opposite temperaments were
not able to exist in pre-eminence together, till the
end of the Coalition era the King was in a backwater.

He persevered. He went on his unostentatious
way. He shewed himself wiser than Lloyd George
about Ireland, and than Asquith about Labour.
When for the first time the Labour Party came to
power, some feared, and some hoped, that the
Monarchy might not play fair with this government of
a new social and political type: the King of course
received, and worked with, his new ministers as
cordially and as impartially as with those of the
older parties. Spontaneously, and put to it by neither

party, he made it a principal royal duty to go about among his poorer subjects, and the factory towns, up and down England. Some of the Tories viewed the new departure with scorn; the Crown was theirs, not the rabble's. Some of the Socialists, preferring a state of discontent, noted with chagrin that the royal solicitude weakened it. In the north and midlands royalty was seen by millions who had never seen, or thought to see, a king.

Kind, kind and gentle is she would greet the King's lady, and pleasure and friendly cheering always. Queen Mary was an unqualified asset. Ladies of the Smart Set made jokes about her clothes and hats; which, considering their own in the '20s, fell rather flat in the end. Among all the world's rulers she was the most regal figure.

Fast folk disdained the Court's middle-class virtues, voted it dowdy, and sighed for something more raffish. A few 'intellectuals' jeered:

> *The King is duller than the Queen :*
> *I found him talking to a Rural Dean*
> *About the joys of district visiting :*
> *The Queen is duller than the King.*

George said he would rather abdicate than sit through *Hamlet* a second time, and had the joke on them.

Nearly the totality of the nation respected,

60

admired and liked these good people doing a good job well. The young Prince of Wales supplied the more romantic and enthusiastic note.

Insensibly, the period of royal effacement came to an end, and by the later twenties the throne was as prominent again as in Edward's heyday. The King's and Queen's own merits were a chief reason; the twilight of the democratic and self-advertising gods, the Wilsons and the Lloyd Georges, another. The new non-monarchical Europe was already revealed a worse failure than its predecessor. The French Revolution was over.

In the small but influential world of the bookish and educated, meanwhile, the appearance of Lytton Strachey's *Queen Victoria* and of the later volumes of the Queen's own Letters stimulated interest in the monarchy; a favourable interest, whatever in the one case the sly author may have at first intended, or some radicals predicted of the other.

It is still near to judge; but the main results of the last reign, monarchically, appear to be three. The Crown became, more clearly, a focal point of national unity at home. It became, much more clearly and powerfully, the symbol of Empire unity. It became, thirdly, the repository, type and example of the virtues the British people most admire in themselves and require of their gods:— charity, kindliness, justice, moderation, common sense;

modesty, integrity; decent and dignified domesticity; unostentatious devotion to duty; unoriginality. In a time and a world where alike astuteness and brute force, lying and licence, showy intellectuality and plain materialism, cynicism and frivolity, were at a rising premium, these still preferred old virtues were the throne's adornment and chief strength. By the end of his reign King George had attained the perfection of the new kingship: simply by being honourably *there*, to be gladly and unanimously accepted as the perfect representative of a great people, nation and empire.

Around the events in the King's life and his Family's, the tendency to regard him as the head of the whole British Family gathered; and shewed force, and acquired it. The Coronation, and the royal progresses following; the installation of the gentle boy-heir as Prince of Wales in Caernarvon Castle; the Durbar; the Declaration of War; Armistice Day, the crowds surging loyally round Buckingham Palace, and when the Guards struck up the National Anthem it was sung with exultation by the people; the unveiling of the Cenotaph, and burial of the Unknown Warrior in the Abbey; the Prince's progresses through the Empire; the successive marriages of the King's other four children; his own illness, and recovery; his Jubilee, the high tide of monarchical enthusiasm in modern history, an enthusiasm sterling and spontaneous, proof of the nation's need to manifest its unity; his death, which called forth an emotion that the exaggerations of the Press and wireless were not able to increase, or even diminish.

Among the complex of causes that made for this crescendo the King's own personality stood first. Without pretension, cleverness or subtlety, without distinguished appearance or personality, he was modest, good-natured and good; he was the antithesis of the trashy, the showy, the brutal, the self-seeking, the false; he was the average *good* English man to the nth.

There was a jest going the rounds some years ago that if all the kings of the earth were suddenly thrown out of their jobs, only two of them would be able to earn their living: the King of England as a dealer in stamps, the King of Italy as an expert on coins. At the new profession of broadcaster, also, King George could have earned his keep. His pure accent was a cruel criticism of those who mostly monopolaize the maicrophone. His voice was perfect and his words so sincere, so modest and so apt to the circumstance that cynicism was rather difficult.

In acknowledgment of his people's Jubilee enthusiasm: "I can only say to you, my very dear people, that the Queen and I thank you from the depth of our hearts for the loyalty and—may I say?—the love with which this day and always you have surrounded us." On Christmas Day of 1935: "How could I fail to note in all the rejoicing not merely respect for the Throne, but a warm and generous remembrance of the man himself who, may God help him, has been placed upon it? It is this personal link between me and my people which I value more than I can say. It binds us together in all our common joys and sorrows, as when this year you showed your happiness in the marriage of my son, and your sympathy in the death of my beloved sister. I feel this link now as I speak to you . . . I add a heartfelt prayer that, wherever you are, God may bless and keep you always."

God had taken him within the month. And if, amid the emotion of sorrow, and while eight hundred thousand of his people passed by and saluted him as he Lay in State, for the first time for over a hundred years there was no tremor of doubt as mysteriously the succession passed, that was due, if in part to the known gifts of his young successor, in greatest part to himself.

When George IV died, *The Times* wrote: "The truth is—and it speaks volumes about the man—that there never was an individual less regretted by his fellow-creatures than this deceased King. What eye has wept for him? What heart has heaved one throb of un-necessary sorrow? If George the Fourth ever had a friend—a devoted friend—in any rank of life—we protest that the name of him or her has not yet reached us."

When George V died, *The Times* wrote: "A reign of great deeds, great sufferings, great perils and great splendour is ended, and the name of King George the Fifth is added to the illustrious roll of those who have loved and lived for their country. . . . All peoples and languages have united with us in reverence for the dead, and even the barriers that political estrangement has raised were as if they had never been when the common human impulse insisted on paying homage to one whose life had done honour to human nature. . . ."

The omens for the new King are favourable. The British peoples ardently desire him.

REPUBLIC

v.

MONARCHY

I

IN this they may be wrong. There is much to be said against monarchy.

It is an offence against human equality. To take one man out from among his fellows, set him on high, place a golden crown upon his head, make of him an idol before which other men bow down, is more than a mummery, comedy, minor absurdity; it is treachery, treachery against the dignity of the human race. This truth is self-evident, that all men are created equal. For Man in his servility to upset God's work and ascribe to one man, created equal with the others, a rank and an essence superior to theirs, is something beyond a mere foible or constitutional fiction; it is a sin against the spirit.

The antique grotesque conventions that still in twentieth-century England govern all intercourse with royalty, the frills and the fawning, the bowing and the bending, perpetuate an inequality of manners. As Manners makyth Man, from outward the vice works inward again and the inequality of Man is confirmed and by these conventions basely strengthened.

It is an offence against reason. To choose the head, if but the titular head, of a civilized modern State by the barbaric hit-and-miss method of hereditary right is illogical, and—had the Englishman but the gift for standing aside to see his complacently admired institutions as they are—ridiculous. The beasts do not choose their rulers according to accident of birth; nor the angels. Nor, almost more relevantly, do the proprietors or shareholders so choose the managing director of a business concern. Why, because his father was his father, should one man have a voice in the government that may outweigh the voice of millions, and into the unequal bargain be honoured and overpaid and kow-towed to for having it?

Ridiculous, the method is chancy. George V's four sons may, by a piece of good luck—good luck at any rate for them—have turned out to be decent average young men; George III had many more than four sons, and there was not a good one among the gang. In countless examples through history bad ruler has succeeded hereditarily unto good, bringing decline or disaster upon his house and, what mattered, his country. Royalty is a risk; at best a relic, a whimsical out-of-date ornament retained because thought scarcely worth abolishing.

It stands against the whole trend of human history. Slowly, with epochs often of apostasy and set-back, Man for long ages has been learning to shake off the trappings of tyranny, the sign and with it the substance of illogical and irresponsible rights: the monarchs and the medicine men, the kings and the priests. England with her king wears in the world the air of an eccentric exception. With the handicap of our snobbery, we are perhaps not yet ripe for a republic; but no land can stand for ever outside the current of natural evolution, to play with such toys all alone.

Twentieth-century paradoxes, calling black white or both grey, cannot alter the known nature of the horrible history of kings. Early they turned to their trade of oppression. They abused the priestly or patriarchal position with which they started, placed there in the tribe's interest and not their own, to acquire military force and political power, and wealth and dominion of fear; and soon everywhere were out of hand, forgetting that kings were made for the people and not the people for the kings. Assyrian and Babylonian monsters of terror, Asshurnazirpal and Shalmaneser, Asshurbanapal and Tiglathpileser, Sargon and Sennacherib, Nebuchadnezzar and Belshazzar; Roman monsters, Caligula and Nero, Commodus and Caracalla and Heliogabalus; Byzantine emperors, Aztec emperors; the stiff sunless glory of the *Roi Soleil*; the old-ogre wickedness of the Kings of Naples, the deformed tragic darkness of the Kings of Spain; Pharaohs, Baals, Ithobaals; nightmare Moguls and Rajahs; Sultans, Shahs, Tsars. . . .

George V, no doubt, was not precisely in the same category as some of these. The modern British Monarchy is less harmful and more human than some variants that history has seen.

In its genteel way it is harmful enough.

Softly and discreetly though the brake works, it is a brake on progress.

Whatsoever the will towards impartiality of this or that individual wearer of it, our Crown inclines always to be a party institution. The evidence is there, fatally abundant in every reign of every English king and queen from the day of the brief and brilliant English Republic up to our own. Charles II and James II were on the side of the Catholics and the divine right party; William III was on the side of the Whigs and the war party. Queen Anne was a blind old Tory; George I and George II were mere hirelings of the Whigs. King George III was a partisan of the King's party, that group of place-hunting Tories who had rallied to the House of Brunswick. First through a favourite such as Lord Bute, later by means of corruption, bribery of Members of Parliament, depriving critics of the Court of posts and pensions and promotion, he governed the country according to his personal royal will, triumphed over ministry after ministry, and lost us the Empire of America. Whether he was more, or less, of an oppressor than his opponents the Whig aristocrats, the enclosing lords, may fairly be debated; but a party man Farmer George was from first to last. George IV, after his Whig youth and princehood, as both Regent and King was a bigoted Tory, able to delay Catholic emancipation and parliamentary

72

reform for dangerous years. William IV ineptly favoured the same side and the same, by then lost, causes. Victoria began as a hot partisan Whig, gradually changed over and continued and ended her unending reign as a hot partisan Conservative; at continual junctures throwing her influence on to the scales for that party and never troubling to conceal from herself, or from Mr. Gladstone, that her party it was.

During the last two reigns, the king's open partisanship has diminished: it has been getting too risky for the king. All the influences around him have remained partisan. Most of a king's personal friends are Tories, most of the people he meets are Tories, the people about the Court and the Town are Tories. The sort of influences around Edward VII may be studied, profitably, in Lord Esher's *Letters*. His Majesty was told that if he created the peers to pass the Parliament Bill, he would "mortally offend the Tory Party, to which he is naturally bound." George V manœuvred against the Parliament Bill, and the Home Rule Bill. In 1931 the downfall of Labour aroused grave suspicions of intrigue on the backstairs of Buckingham Palace. The 'National' Government was born of a Palace Revolution.

In foreign affairs, the English king has a power elastic and therefore dangerous. Victoria exercised continual influence on external policy, commonly against liberty, whenever quietly possible in the private interests of her kin. Edward, as the world

knows—as in 1914 the world saw—meddled assi-
duously in international business. George refused to
receive or shake hands with the accredited representative of a great country, thus heartening the
reactionary forces who were fighting against good
relations with Republican Russia.

The fighting officers' oath is to the King, not the
country. There is real peril here; even if some
distinction can perhaps be made, in our minds and
theirs, between marching regiments and crack cavalry
regiments or the Guards. Closely associated with
the army and the navy—

Slaughter coupled to the name of kings

in particular with the high officers of both, the
monarchy has no such near association with the
country's non-killing services, health, education, the
sciences and arts. "All the hell of monarchy, which
has crushed mankind with its calamities, exactions,
massacres and wars."

It is bound up with the House of Lords, that other
hereditary anomaly, and with privilege generally.

It shares its private relaxations with the small idle
class that does not work, the very rich. The Tory
party is not exclusively a party of the rich; millions
of poor, and poorish, people vote for it and there are
rich men who, out of idealism or vanity or self-
interest, support its opponents. But with rich men,
as with Tories—nineteen times out of twenty they

are the same—the Crown has most to do. Victoria
and George never indeed sought them out, as Edward
did; whose pleasure in the company of ultra-wealthy
foreigners was not always reflected upon with
pleasure by his mere subjects. Those friendships of
his were described, by the plutocratic, as 'democratic.' They were one of the most, among many,
undemocratic things about him.

The King necessarily lives the life of a rich man
himself. He is the apex of a system based on wealth,
that is on poverty; bound up with that system, a
powerful prop of it and gilded guarantee of its continuance. Seeing him there at the head of it, simple
people the more easily persuade themselves that the
system is natural and right.

Monarchy stimulates snobbery.

We the English are born snobs enough already:
flunkeys, as Cobden called us, from first to last. But
this king business adds its extra spice of nastiness and
a measure of political importance to the social pride
of the powerful; it encourages a gushing admiration
for their betters among the poor and ignorant, who
gape at the royal pictures in the newspapers or as the
kingly cortège goes by.

> Oh, 'tis the sweetest of all earthly things
> To gaze on Princes and to talk of Kings.

Place, pride, titles, the love of mean things, are
fostered and exalted by this consecrated supreme

75

example of them, Majesty the Gaudy Name. Daily and lavishly the theme is 'featured' by the millionaire Press which shrewdly, deliberately and politically exploits it. The more opulent weekly illustrateds descend to a dark low-level of sycophancy; and their most craven captions are in adulation of the Royal Family, when not of that hard-faced smart crowd (the unpleasantest people in England) who while regarding the Family as proprietarily theirs are the first to gossip, sneer and salaciously snigger about and against it.

Upon the minds of much pleasanter people a senile pall comes down when royalty is scented. Judgment goes blind; the irrational note triumphs; every voice is hushed.

In this atmosphere of awed unreality, royalty has prospered. The Jubilees of Queen Victoria were an enormous unreality, bad for the worshipped, worse for the weak heads of the worshippers: how little there was in common between the idealized Great White Queen and the obscurantist fat little woman of pig-headed fact. The hot-tempered, rather coarse, not very intelligent man of the world called Edward VII became, in dying, a combination and culmination of the talents and virtues of half the high figures of history: became Solon, Socrates, Sir Galahad, Saint Francis, Machiavelli, Abraham Lincoln all in one. George V was extolled beyond all resemblance to his homely merits; while the Marina madness and the

Jubilee junketings displayed, as they encouraged, the intellectual debility of a people of lackeys. Face to face with royalty, values go wrong.

Queen Alexandra, when Princess of Wales, walked lame after an illness; at once hundreds of servile or ambitious ladies developed 'the Alexandra limp.' Edward VII, when Prince of Wales, had one day finished his after-luncheon cup of coffee at an hotel, and walked out; in rushed a lady, snatched the cup and triumphantly drank down the dregs. Men it was, as well as women, who another time knelt down and picked up and sacramentally consumed the crumbs that had fallen from his table, and on yet another occasion fought for and sucked clean the duck-bones Edward had left on his princely plate. What the sex of the king-worshipper who, by loyal waiting and watching, had the high inspiring experience of using the privy next immediately after His Royal Highness, may be left in lenient obscurity.

In modern England, amid the multifarious pressing problems of social and political reorganization which face her, the royal pageantry is a dangerous distraction; diverting men's minds, with still a disheartening degree of success, from matters that matter.

> To-day in Britain Demos rules
> And we, some forty million fools
> With Pomp and Parliament are fed.
> We've got the circus. Where's the bread?

77

The old republican jingle is not less relevant to-day, with misery abroad as ever in the land.

The throne, a party and class institution, is a very local institution also; a thing of London, where it spends most of its money and holds most of its shows, and—Windsor, Ascot, Sandringham—of the spineless degenerate counties round about. Outside the south-eastern quarter of one of the kingdoms it wears an alien air, and is seen for the rich man's toy and tool that it is. Ask them in Durham, in Glamorgan, on Clydeside.

The necessity of the Crown as the 'imperial link' is exaggerated. It is a parrot-cry. The Dominions retain their membership of the British Empire first because it is their interest to do so, second for reasons such as habit, sentiment, the language bond. It reveals an odd sense of fundamental values to imagine that a bauble holds a great Empire together. In one of the Dominions, South Africa, there is general and in another, Ireland, almost universal sentiment for a republic. In the remaining Dominions, with possibly the small and too-English exception of New Zealand, monarchy is a very fragile bloom.

In so far as he is not actively harmful, the king is a superfluous fiction. His executive powers are exercised by others. His ceremonial doings are useless when not pernicious.

It is a mere chance that he has survived so long; many times from George I to George V it has been

touch-and-go. Unfortunately, the longer the institution manages to hold out the stronger is English
obstinacy in its favour likely to become. Its survival,
we tell ourselves, is proof of our national genius for
combining tradition with common sense, or other
self-flattery of the sort; the survival continuing,
our belief in our genius grows stronger—and the
thing's chance of yet further survival.

Last, the Cost. *The salary of the King of England is
£410,000; of the President of the United States, £15,000.*

Figures don't lie.

Add the fat pensions and perquisites of the princes,
and all the incidental waste and unsocial spending
the thing involves: the shows, the gold braid; the
money squandered, and pocketed only by luxury
milliners and their like, on the dressing of débutantes,
on royal weddings, jubilees, coronations and the
rest.

Is it worth it?

Such considerations are, in these deferent days,
hardly given a hearing. Our ancestors were freer men.

They are in part negative considerations. There is
the positive enthusiasm, the purest and most passionate in history, for the Republic.

That word has been a clarion call, summoning men
to cast off their chains, rise up and destroy the
oppressor, fling into limbo all the lumber of thrones
and altars, and under the pure name be free. For it,

humanity's heroes have died: Harmodius and Aristo-
giton, Arnold of Brescia and Cola di Rienzo, Sidney,
Mazzini. Under its glorious sign—

> . . . *the fair*
> *And fierce Republic with the feet of fire*—

the young tattered armies of liberated France
advanced to meet the despots, and defied and scat-
tered them all. In its name, a shade more soberly,
Englishmen across the Atlantic founded the mightiest
democratic State of history. For its sake, throughout
the century of the Revolution men were inspired,
and lived more nobly, and toiled and fought more
bravely to shake off tyranny and ancient wrong. It is
the one mysterious symbol that is not on the
oppressor's side. It is the one ideal idol. Whoso has
never once felt the thrill of the word Republic has
not loved liberty enough.

Accidents of our peculiar national history and temperament have made the word speak to the blood of
Englishmen less imperiously, with less force of
triumphant idealism and divine contagion; and, so
far, no lasting fruits. The difference can be, and in
this reactionary day always is, overstated. Republicanism in England is a fine and neglected chapter in
the story of human aspiration after liberty.

The old Puritans first fought the good fight.
Jehovah's judgment done upon our shiftiest king,

there began the eleven unservile years of our story: Oliver made an England from which the trash and the trumpery were cleared away. Man's lower ways are powerful ways; and the prince and the pimps came back. They dug up the great Protector's body, to defile it, and his old mother's—the Cavalier gentlemen that they were. Algernon Sidney kept the pure flag flying. He looked at the outwardly brilliant French Monarchy and said: The beauty of it is false and painted; and, prophetically, Its starving and desperate people will one day make an end. He looked at Charles Stuart's own Court, and told them: Monarchy is founded on human depravity. They took him, and murdered him; the last Englishman to die on the scaffold for the Republic. After the long sordid eighteenth century, idealism awoke again and the great poets, Shelley and the young Wordsworth and Byron and Landor, in darkest days of Regency and reaction preached the kingless Word. In prose as in practice (two other countries he helped to free), brave Tom Paine, one of the most unjustly belittled men in the English annals, fought in the same cause. Burke beheld France in revolution and could only pity the plumage: Paine remembered the dying bird.

They were beaten. And their successors, alike the idealists who descended from Sidney and Shelley and the plain-reason men in the tradition of Tom Paine, were beaten: by the massed forces of nineteenth-century materialism gathered around the appropriate throne of Queen Victoria. To our cheap and cynical age they look dingy and rather comical now, those earnest-eyed artisans of the grimy industrial towns who hearkened to Bradlaugh and believed that there was something in a name, and that one name spelt delusion and ancient wrong and the Other Name a higher way for men and women and a fairer age for the world.

They failed. But the flame that burned in them—

Light of the light of man,
Reborn republican—

may flare forth even again; and sweep England yet.

II

Human equality is a thing that has never existed. The capitalists, the owners and masters, the slave-drivers, who foregathered at Philadelphia in 1776 were strange people to imagine that it did. This truth indeed is self-evident, that men are not created equal. Neither in strength, nor brains, nor beauty; nor in bodily health nor spiritual worth; nor in anything between the common bournes of birth and death. The most that human governance can do, in the rare brief periods of human history when it so desires, is to diminish somewhat the number and the severity of the hardships which this given inequality must involve. As a cadre for such diminishing, monarchy is nowhere a form of government less favourable than any republics revealed to us. Has the Jew as they flog him to death with rubber truncheon, the bourgeois tortured and shot by order of Red tribunal, the black man burnt alive amid democratic American laughter at the pitiless stake, heart to rejoice that he is Citizen of a Republic, time or tears to spare from his own agony for the degraded poor lackeys of a monarchy like ours? Republic, if ever it had, has no longer any greater connotation of equality; or freedom, or justice, or humanity. The best-governed countries in the world are the constitutional monarchies: our own, with Holland, Sweden, and a few others. The worst-governed are all republics.

Compared to over-great wealth, an over-powerful party or police, chattel slavery or wage slavery, deification of race or State or hate, kingship is a puny theoretical offence against this equality that never has been. It can offend logic-choppers, whom such abstract ills have power to offend. A Frenchman, naturalised English, told an Englishman that the only reason he regretted his change of nationality was that he had ceased to be citizen of a republic and had become the subject of a king. It offended his sense of human dignity. In France there was no such attaint on dignity and equality; none.

"Brothels?" suggested priggishly the Englishman.

The ex-Frenchman smiled pityingly. "There's no comparison," he said.

"None," replied the Englishman.

Kingship is the form of government that goes not most, but least, against common sense. What more intelligible than a human point of political union: rule *personified?* All history has understood this form better. We understand it better, and our white dominions, and our humble coloured fellow-subjects throughout the continents. During the War there were those African chiefs who refused to renew their contracts to serve until they succeeded in doing so in the presence of King George himself; at Abbeville I remember it was. The majority of his five hundred million subjects do not know what a Parliament is: Him they can understand.

Most men, most of the time, are not fond of government. Monarchy is a means of securing respect and affection for it. Contrast England and France. A means of combining the benefits of tradition with the benefits of freedom.

Election is not the better way. We do not elect our judges, our jurymen; our civil servants, our military officers; our fathers, our gods. A king being chosen as it were by lot—the pure chance of heredity—the chance is that an average decent man will turn up; the majority of men being, by definition, average and, by any cheerful view of human nature,

84

decent. Chance will inflict rarely upon us a criminal or a clown—George III's brood was a run on the black that is unlikely soon to repeat itself—and we could set him aside painlessly if it did.

There is more than the negative advantage of chance. Chance gives birth to the king, but—wise policy then takes over. He is trained for his destiny; trained, as in no other profession, from birth. Our British hereditary president is brought up every hour with a view to fitting him for his future duties. It is elected presidents who are chancy. They may have been brought up to become anything; or nothing. In fitness for their job, by what discernible standards have the four Britannic sovereigns of the last century been inferior to the contemporary presidents of the republics? Examine the French list, the Haitian; the Liberian, the American. Presidential Conventions in the States do not look for a good president, they look for a good candidate; which is rather rarely the same thing. By accident it may once in a way turn out to be, and so even republics sometimes get good rulers. As when the bosses, on that famous day at Chicago in 1860, did their usual deal and stumbled on the noble tremendous accident of Abraham Lincoln.

These rulers picked by reason and the People do not seem to be so safe at the hands of either as our hereditary monsters. World-Saviour Wilson, when he drove through London with Tyrant George, was surprised—ay, and damned anxious—because no

detectives rode on the footboard of the royal car. Of
the last fifteen Presidents of the United States three
have been assassinated; or one in five. Of the last ten
Presidents of the French Republic, two; the same
proportion. In each country, one every twenty years.
Of the sovereigns of England since Bosworth Field,
one—by the Republic—has met a violent death. One
in twenty. One in four hundred years.

The trend of human history? Nothing is known
of it.

To think that because England is now the exception, it must be exception to a rule that is good—
to pronounce her not 'ripe' for a republic—is brazen
begging the question. Are Germany, Austria, Hungary, Brazil, Spain better off now than when they
were monarchies? Is post-War republican Europe a
happier or a more prosperous or a freer or a more
peace-loving place, now that nationality or race are
its gods in the stead of the old emperors and kings?

Our throne, a brake on progress? If progress
should mean the tendency, in so far as there is one,
towards fairer social conditions, milder yet more
efficient government, more tolerance and justice, a
bigger chance for a fuller life for a larger number
of the people, if it should mean anything that the
word might sanely mean, then there is no evidence
that the existence of, or any aim or action of, the
British monarchy is a brake upon it. Most of the
republics have the brakes full on all right.

The abuse of kings, the abuse of the word king, is a verbal inheritance from one short period in history: the period of the decaying absolute monarchies; of the English Revolution, the 'Enlightenment,' the French Revolution; with the brilliant anti-royalist writing that preceded, accompanied and followed, that partly caused and wholly glorified those movements. Man is wolf to man; with the power finds pleasure in doing his brother harm. The danger of every form of government becoming oppressive government is perpetual. Monarchy being the most eminent example of man's power over man, and the usual form of government through history, *kings* was easily turned into a stock symbol of oppression.

In a majority of lands, the Other Side to monarchy has been not the people but the people's enemies: barons, feudal lords, the local tyrant, the usurer, the soldier. The king has been the general avenger of the poor, the weak, the wronged. The King's Peace. I appeal unto Cæsar. To-day, the wolves are at it as gaily as ever: how many of them are kings?

In committing the injustices for which they are most famous, or infamous, kings have commonly been the faithful interpreters of their people. George III was not more anti-Catholic than England, or Louis XIV more anti-Protestant than France; Philip II was not more pro Catholic than Spain, Elizabeth (in her simulation) not more pro-Protestant than England.

87

The party prejudice of the British crown at many moments between the Great Rebellion and the death of Queen Victoria is not in dispute. But since? Which of the two parties did Edward VII cleave to; or, of the three, George V?

The King naturally did not *desire*—nor did his Prime Minister—to create those hordes of Parliament Bill Peers, but he accepted Asquith's advice and decided that he would do it if he had to; if the Opposition and the Government between them made it unavoidable. The constitutional position was abnormal. The Government had no mandate for Home Rule; the House of Lords controversy did not interest the people as it did the politicians; in England proper the majority was on the other side. However unattractive Ulster and the ranting leader of Ulster appeared to many, their disloyalty was a highly special kind of disloyalty: it was loyalty to the Union they belonged to. In such an imbroglio, some intervention of the impartial Crown was natural, as it was necessary.

Throughout the first crisis it was not the kings, Edward then George, who were partisan; rather the Government which tried to impose fundamental change it had no honest mandate for, or the Opposition which was enraged with the kings for *not* being partisan, and for daring to accept their constitutional advisers' advice. They, the fortunate and fashionable circles of London, the West End and the clubs, were the anti-royalists; denouncing the exercise of the royal prerogative; because it was going for once to be used against them. They it was, a year or two later, who hoped the King would go back to Queen Anne's time, revive the veto, and refuse assent to the Home Rule Bill. Asquith pointed out that, in that case, the Liberals when in opposition would have the right to expect the King to reject Conservative bills *they* did not like. If the King intervened once on one side, he would have to intervene another time on the other side; and go on intervening. The Crown would be entering very troubled waters.

King George, like a good sailor, kept out of them.

Neither party made his task too easy. The extreme elements on both sides never will. Violent Tories get disloyal if the King is not on their side; violent Radicals are always suspecting that he may be. Give thanks for the royal brake on violence, and be glad that England has, whether Labour Governments or Conservative Governments, always His Majesty's Government, with the moderating results the mere magical name of the thing helps to secure.

Who solemnly believes that 1931 was a 'Palace Revolution'? Who besides Mr. Laski, Mr. Woolf? Other lands there are, kingless, in which those two able men would for their ability (for their views, their blood) be prisoners, or kicked pariahs, or dead meat. Their hair-splitting little grievances against the hospitable King of England seem inelegant therefore;

ungrateful almost; an untimely instance of the patho-
logical lack of perspective of their brilliant race.

In foreign affairs the sovereign's say is slight. Since
about 1890, princely kinships have played small part
in his interests, and have had no bearing on policy.
Edward did not conceive the entente with France,
though when his ministers had decided upon it he
eminently helped them to achieve it. What man,
George or other, would have shaken hands with the
envoy of the government that had so foully murdered
his friend and first cousin? A first cousin once
removed, the young Prince of Wales, took on the
distasteful duty and clasped the Red hand.

Better if his say were not so slight—for all our
sakes, and our children's, and the miserable world's!
Versailles had been a saner scrap of paper, a little less
consciously and competently the Peace to end Peace,
if the kings instead of the dreadful democratic tribunes
had still counted, and could have brought their relative
sanity to bear. Queen Victoria would *most* emphatically have declined to *allow* anything so *disgraceful*
as Versailles.

It is a vicious circle, of course. In the air of hate
which Europe breathes to-day the Republic, the
regime of demagogic mass nationalism and mania, is
the natural form. Kings cannot breathe that air. The
very name Victoria conjures up a vision of a more
civilized age, a golden age long past, in which
madness and murder of the 1937 level of republican

intensity would not have been even understood.

If our King, one of the few surviving from that better day, had retained the same right as of old to be effectively informed about foreign affairs, more than one recent incident humiliating to England and dangerous to all could never have occurred. With an amatcur Prime Minister, King's control is the more necessary: he would insist that all international affairs of importance be weighed, carefully, by the whole Cabinet. Our governments being usually elected on home policy, the King is our safeguard against their making a great change in international policy they have no mandate for.

The King is naturally the head of the army and the navy; as are the presidents of the republics red, black or white. A sovereign institution less military in tone, less belligerent in its known influence, than the modern British Monarchy it would be hard to discover or invent. Edward the Peacemaker, if the surname was optimistic, tried in Europe as he tried in Ireland—and as he had succeeded in South Africa, and among his own friends all his life—to stop strife continually. In civilian clothes he looked one of the best-dressed men in Europe, but far from impressive in uniform. The Family to-day has its chief interest in the peaceful activities of the nation.

The throne is in no way bound up with the Lords. Against, as for, that remarkable chamber there are some good arguments and some bad ones; all equally irrelevant here. The two institutions have nothing in common except the hereditary principle, which applies to the Lords but partially. The Lords are a party body; the King is above party. The Crown is an executive and ceremonial headship functioning under the guidance of each successive Cabinet; the Lords are a caste of legislators who favour Cabinets of one colour. The heir to the throne is trained for his job, under Cabinet control; the Peers educate their heirs, if at all, as they please. They have no obligations; the King has only obligations. The Crown is the head of a world empire; the Lords are the quaint privilege of our island alone.

The King, it is true, does not live in grinding poverty. Nor did Lenin. Overcrowded though Buckingham Palace is said to be, he does not live in a slum. He gets enough to eat. So does Stalin. Of our last four sovereigns, three—an unfamiliar proportion for presidents of republics—have been conspicuously not partial to the company of the very rich. Monarchy is the negation of plutocracy. It is one of the few remaining things in this world not based upon and not buyable with money.

The effect on public life is salutary. In the republics, as Montrose said long ago, the great ones strive for the garland; in monarchies, as Disraeli added, the prize of supreme place stands high outside the sphere of human passions and ambitions.

The Crown is so little bound up with the present

economic system that its continuance is consistent
with the total disappearance of that system or with
any intermediate reform of it. If England went
Bolshevik we could, and quite likely should, keep the
king. His Majesty's Soviets.

Snobbery. To honour an august and historic
tradition, to venerate the emblem that has stood for
England for over one thousand years, is not snobbery.
Not to respect and honour it is snobbery. Even were
snobbery the price to pay for our king, how tiny a
price: for our royal freedom from hysteria, beastliness, political murder, oppression, hate. If the King
is not the cause of our freedom from these evils, he
is a symptom of it. If the throne fell, these things
would probably come upon us. If they came upon
us, the throne would go.

Anyone who thinks that there is less admiration
of things other than for their intrinsic worth under
a republic, can know very little of republican history,
or of history. There is a White House snobbery. There
is an Elysée snobbery. There is a Kremlin snobbery.
Its American counterparts out-Tatler *The Tatler*.

The duck-bone snatchers and suckers, the coffee-
dregs drinker, were snobs by almost any definition.
Only: they were not the subjects of a monarchy.
They were citizens one and all of a great free
Republic across the seas.

Our own rather less exuberant delight in the
King, with all its cheap exaggerations, is I think on

balance a credit entry; bound up with that respect for respectable things and that absence of social envy which are among our sounder national qualities. One Court night I watched the crowd, a crowd of poor people, that was waiting outside Buckingham Palace to see the débutantes and the diplomats in their finery stream out. There was much audible comment, one old Cockney lady in particular addressing the great ones with racy banter and giving them, as they stepped to their carriages, her decided views about their raiment and their personal appearance; but no faint sign of jealousy, or of ill-feeling at the contrast between the luxury of the courtiers and the poverty of the beholders. To apostles of the Revolution such a frame of mind must be distressing. It struck me, a fellow-subject as unlikely ever to go to Court as any other members of that crowd, in its good humour as English and admirable. If rather more than anyone deserves.

Men (and women) want *circenses* as well as *panem*. These the throne provides, cheaply and harmlessly; with no background of terror. Our Royal shows are good shows, with the advantage of having a meaning, a high and historic meaning. You won't change the English. Back in the Middle Ages they were as keen on having, and seeing, their royal festivities as now. The sacrists' rolls at Westminster Abbey show that long centuries ago the Belfry was let, most profitably, to sightseers at the Coronation tournaments.

94

The King is not an irrelevant distraction from pressing problems. He is rather a guarantee of their peaceful solution. The republic is irrelevant.

The throne has never been less a mere London throne than to-day: Edward VIII knows Durham, Glamorgan, Clydeside. It is the Parliament in London and the complacency of London that the neglected provinces resent: the isle of fatness in a lean land, for which the Government does little, the King at least what he can.

The Crown's imperial importance cannot be exaggerated. Of the British Empire, the great free alliance of the least unfree peoples in the world, it is at once the symbol and practical bond. Enlightened self-interest is one of the two links of Empire; the Crown is the other. Of the two the Crown is not the weaker.

The Mother of Parliaments having relinquished her supreme jurisdiction over the Dominions, the Crown is now the only political link. The Governors-General no longer represent Westminster but the King. Overseas statesmen visiting London are likelier to know one of the royal princes than one of the Cabinet Ministers.

The influence, pathetically slight, that the King of the Empire has in the terrible issue of race and colour is thrown always on to the side of justice and mercy. He cannot forget that he is king equally of all his subjects, whatever the tint of their skins.

When the Crown took over the government of India, Lord Derby submitted to Queen Victoria the proclamation to the Indian peoples that he had prepared. She wrote back that the tone was not friendly enough, not warm enough: "Such a document should breathe feelings of generosity, benevolence, and religious toleration." She made the minister change it, change it into one of the finest proclamations of her reign, or any reign: "Firmly relying ourselves on the truth of Christianity, we disclaim alike the right and the desire to impose our convictions on any of our subjects. We declare it to be our royal will and pleasure that none be in any wise favoured, none molested or disquieted by reason of their religious faith or observances, but that *all shall alike enjoy the equal and impartial protection of the law*. And we do strictly charge and enjoin all those who may be in authority under us that they abstain from all interference with the religious belief or worship of any of our subjects on pain of our highest displeasure." She may have been an out-of-date old frump, and queenship a queer and comical survival, but can one imagine the Leader of the brilliant up-to-date German Republic issuing such a proclamation—can one?

After the Mutiny the Queen stood out strongly against retaliation and the rabid cries for vengeance. "There is," she declared to the Governor-General, "no hatred of a brown skin, *none*." She may have been a hidebound old reactionary, and monarchism an anachronism, but can one imagine the President of the great American Republic, where all men are free and equal, going south of the Mason-Dixon line and making such a declaration—can one?

Edward VII inherited her strong dislike of racial oppression and discrimination. On his Indian tour of 1876, as a young man (a mere wastrel) he wrote to her: "The rude and rough manner in which the English 'political officers' treat the natives is quite wrong. Natives of all classes in this country will be more attached to us if they are treated with kindness, and firmness at the same time, but not with brutality and contempt." He had the fullest pride in Englishmen's mighty achievement in India, but saw and pilloried their major blemish. To Lord Granville he wrote: "Because a man has a black face and a different religion from our own, there is no reason why he should be treated like a brute"; and to Lord Salisbury, of "the disgraceful habit of speaking of niggers." Royal deeds followed royal words; one of the worst offenders, the Resident in Hyderabad, was recalled to England; and though the cads took umbrage, decent Anglo-Indian opinion responded. As King he urged the same views; he was King-Emperor of the hard-worked incorruptible British official and of the dusky native alike. Colour cruelty he would not condone in brother-kings' dominions either, and holding Leopold personally responsible for the Congo abominations (which he was), despite the latter's persistent whinings to be received declined ever to meet him.

Last, the Cost.

Figures lie. Of the King's nominal £410,000, Edward has voluntarily and generously forgone a part, using the revenues of his own private Duchy of Cornwall to relieve the taxpayer; another large part would be variously incurred in any event, king or no king, and quite aside from the cost of the unknown institution which would replace him. Many things which our king has to pay for out of his wage are paid for the President of the United States on other items of the American budget than his salary. Add the corruption, the jobbing, the waste, the horde of incoming placemen that each change-over in the national headship there involves. The cost of the American elections in the upset of trade alone, in presidential year, has been estimated at four million dollars, or double the King's salary.

France does it cheaper; as she does most things, has to, likes to. But totting up the salaries of the President and household, and items elsewhere in the French budget which the King of England carries on his civil list, and the cost of the election, and the cost of corruption, perhaps—perhaps—Edward VIII may cost us a few thousands a year more.

He costs us, to ignore outside comparisons, about one fiftieth of one per cent of our Budget; or, taking the Privy Purse alone and deducting the probable expenditure on that improbable British President, *.00008* of our national expenditure.

He is worth it.

The word Republic, which most Englishmen contrive to utter as prose instead of poetry, has a long and interesting history. It is an outstanding example of an undescriptive and immobile name for a various and changing thing. It denotes States and forms of government so diverse that it is very nearly without meaning. What is there in common between the tiny town-state of antiquity and the federal continent of ultra-modernity, between the Athenian and American republics, except that both had no hereditary head and that both were founded on slavery? Since one of the two has abolished the latter and given its Chief of State more than monarchical powers, what single bond of likeness is there between them? Or between a peasant and *petit bourgeois* federation like Switzerland and a closed city-aristocracy like Venice? The United States is the most powerful unit in the world, San Marino the feeblest. There are autocratic republics, and there are democratic ones. There is Plato's Republic, and there is Hitler's.

The truest republics of history are the headless city-states of the ancient world: immortal Athens, Thebes, Corinth. The citizens, that small minority who had political power, were intelligent enough—

in some ways the most intelligent people who ever have lived—to question the right of any one intelligence among them to be raised to rule over them. They were logical enough to split kingship up into its various logical parts: the priestly, the administrative, the executive, the ornamental. Their States were small enough for them to be conscious, uniquely conscious, of their statehood without the need of any symbol of it. Brilliant the Hellenic cities were. Miserably in politics they failed. Down the tiny rickety structures went. Empire englobed them.

In later days the headless State has been tried again, and has always perished. The practical difficulties have proved too great. With the growing size and anonymity of States, a personal vision of sovereignty is more needed than before, and this monarchies provide better than the republics; which as a rule afford less freedom and justice, furnish worse government and suffer from greater corruption than the monarchies. They are likelier to fall into the hands of rich cliques.

In England the Word has no magic. The republican enthusiasm, if respectable, has been shared in our country by a tiny eccentric minority, aside from the main current of the national story. It is a very tenuous, bookish tradition. Milton and Harrington, as republicans, are not more than literary curiosities. Shelley and Swinburne were poetizing; their dreams, clothed in matchless words, had no relation to realities and Swinburne's not even to meaning. There is no continuous tradition. The 1689 revolution snapped it, and Tom Paine's was a new start. An importation also; in England republicanism has always seemed a foreign article.

The leading advocates of the alien form have, at all periods, been for the most part men of poor or unattractive character, or of shallow conviction, or opponents of working-class claims and reforms that mattered. The incorruptible Algernon Sidney, stripped of the fair clothing in which Whig propaganda had decked him, is the traitor who took cash (a thousand guineas) from the French Ambassador, and the criminal who paid cash (though rather less) for the foul libels of Titus Oates. Tom Paine, like Jack Wilkes, like Charlie Dilke, had a private life which, however emotionally stimulating, did not specifically fit him to lead a crusade against the effete corruptions of monarchy. Brougham, the chief Regency radical, who talked of playing football with kings' heads, talked with equal enthusiasm of "reducing the labourer to a coarser kind of food." He deplored the expensiveness of George IV, and himself by way of pension plundered the country to the tune of one hundred thousand pounds. The 1870 people were second-rate. They changed their opinions rather too quickly when the wind changed: Chamberlain and his cronies. Swinburne dwindled from a republican poet into a jingo poetaster. Honest

John Morley lived to take a title and pirouette in Court dress. To-day, in 1937, the dozen or so men in England—publicists, professors, politicians—to whom anti-king sentiment is attributed are not men to whom an attractive, or a humble, character is in all cases attributed also. Gnawed by the inferiority complex, most of them; devoured by neurotic vanity.

Kingship has had the heroes; and the more illustrious and constructive history. The nations that we are, that rose on the ruins of Rome, all found their unity around their point of unity the King. Kings made England, France, Spain. Germany lacked her national monarch, and has had a miserable and distracted history. It is the main tradition of Christian Europe. Jesus Christ was born under a monarchy. It is the national tradition of England.

We've had our Republic, and we know. Despite the Whig and Puritan case so ceaselessly and brilliantly for generations drummed into us, the memory of the Commonwealth in popular tradition is bad. Despite the cult of the Cromwells who are ruling half Europe to-day, it will continue bad. The likeness of Oliver and his Commonwealth to Adolf and his Third Reich is, if incomplete, less arbitrary than the average of historical analogy: the personal sincerity and hysteria of the man, the pure and the perverted idealism of the movement, the patriotism and the terror. There are differences. Hitler persecutes the Jews; Cromwell brought them back, but persecuted almost everybody else. Hitler is broad based upon at least a large mass of his public opinion; Cromwell trembled uneasily upon the support of a tiny minority, ruling by spies and the sword alone. Precisely as regards those aspects in which republics are claimed, by republicans, to be superior—personal liberty, equal justice, the sovereignty of the general will, the supremacy of the civilian over the military, peace— the English Republic is the blackest period in our story.

It was the rule of a fanatic fraction, on top by brute force. Any risings, whether of the majority against the tyranny of the minority, or of sections of the minority who disagreed with the Leader, were quelled savagely. He sent brave opponents to the Barbados, as after Worcester he sold the Scots prisoners for the Guinea gold mines at half a crown a dozen. To whisper even against the despotism meant gaol, the sledge, the gallows. No breath of liberty stirred. The soldiery ruled and ravaged. From the Republic dates the English hatred of military power; Oliver conferred at least that unintentional benefit upon us, and guaranteed the unmilitary character of our government ever since. Flattery, supposedly a defect of monarchies—flattery such as the wretched Charles had never lent ear to—was heaped upon the rich men who had murdered him: the mighty Milton laid it on with a majestic trowel. The despot strode in with his musketeers and roughs to disband the representatives of the people, and got rid of three Reichstags running with a brutal competence the timid Charles would have declined, though he might have envied. Taxation, to get money for the soldiery, and for his secret service (God's Gestapo), and for himself, he pushed to heights the frugal Charles had not dared to dream of; and "Thorough" to depths Strafford would have shrunk from. Ferocious laws, such as have never been known in England before or since, were enacted and ferociously enforced. Each kind of tyranny that had been attributed by the rich men his enemies to the mild misgovernment of Charles was repeated by his successor their representative, and intensified past recognition and soon past bearing; and many new kinds. Each of his cruelties he made fouler by blasphemy: "I am persuaded that this [the cruelty] is a righteous judgment of God." Superstition rose to black fury. Hitler of Huntingdon must have his own Witch-Finder-General, and hundreds of poor helpless old women were tortured and drowned.

The march of the Republic through Ireland is the worst stain on the English name. It was an orgy of bestial killing. "I think that night," gloats the villain in his despatch after Drogheda, "they put to the sword about 2000 men. I forbade them to spare any." Those poor wretches that took refuge in the steeple of St. Peter's Church he gave the personal order to have burned alive. Their cries of agony were sweet music in his ears. He heard them, the old Saint and sadist licked his lips and transcribed them: God damn me, God confound me, *I burn, I burn*. He robbed the Irish of their land, their country; murdered their devoted priests and friars, incited his ruffianly mercenaries to take no prisoners; ordered butchery, butchery everywhere, in cold blood; and sent slave-raiding for girls. He may have won us Jamaica; he lost us Ireland for ever.

"Nine men in England out of ten are against you," said Edmund Calamy bravely to his face. "What if I put a sword into the tenth man's hand?" was the answer; and the cowed land was parcelled out into military provinces under the heel of his Major-Generals. Courts martial replaced the courts. Delation was erected into a system, village by village, and for the only time in its history England was ruled by spies. To protect his own precious person against the fury of the people, the dragooned and almost unanimous people who wanted peace, freedom and their King, in brave republican fashion he took to wearing a coat of mail under his dress. He died before they could get him. He died unrepentant. He was a devout Christian, a great original person, the finest cavalry leader in our history, and a sounder imperialist than all the Stuarts added together. He destroyed the King of England, who soon rose from the dead and was stronger. He destroyed the republic of England without hope or desire of resurrection.

III

All which bandied pros and cons, squared absolutes of preference or prejudice, and all the opinions (here sacrificed) that Aristotle and Aquinas and the ancients, and Machiavelli and Montesquieu and the moderns, have delivered upon the issue are, if of slight possible interest to some few people who do not matter, of no interest whatever to any who do:— to the average Englishman; to the political parties.

As a party issue the Crown, if in no other way, is dead.

Within each party, no doubt, there are nuances. Although, within the great Conservative Party, that anti-royalist ardour which pursued Queen Victoria with bad manners through her first two or three decades is as dead as the party's older-time Jacobitism, and neither survives in more than a few isolated families, and although the High Whigs who swelled the party in Home Rule days are less Whiggish about kings than they were, yet here is by no means the nest of loyalty unconditioned that is imagined, and boasted; and at the Tory door may lie the Monarchy's chief peril ahead. Unchastened spirits in those ranks it is who claim the King as their own—as they claim the Union Jack, and the Empire, and England, and the patriotic virtues, and the simple ones. They it is who seek to exploit him in the interests of the

Interests; who assume he must always be on their side, and would use him as ally and instrument; who would drag him, for their private advantage, into the class and party struggle.

This generation has seen some unashamed instances. It was a Tory peer, not a Socialist agitator, who roundly stated that if King George took the advice of his (Liberal) ministers, "the allegiance of a great number of people would be lost." It was middle-class Unionists, gun-running behind the Carsons and the parsons, who described his correct attitude towards Irish policy as "kissing the Scarlet Woman" and George the kisser as a fellow with "not a drop of English blood in his veins." It was "loyal" Orangemen, not low republicans or Reds, who threatened to "kick the King's crown into the Boyne."

Such lively reminders of the limits of Tory loyalty are not out of place, or time; years very near ahead may see instances more unashamed, and more important. If Labour ever tries to put Labour policy seriously into practice and its hand deep into rich men's pockets, and if then the King does *not* (by veto, dissolution or other such action as will be desired of him) take sides with privilege, the limits of that famous loyalty will—as under Charles I, James II, George I, George V—once again be seen, and heard. Down with the Traitor King!

This is not quite fantastic.

Only, it is not quite fair. The old party is the

champion of more than money-bags. Royalty fits in
with all that is best in the Tory creed: love of tradition, stability, dignity, glory; patriotic pride, the
sentiment of personal loyalty and fidelity; preference
for moderation and ordered English progress; dislike of
violence, rash experiment, pointless change; the good
of all the great nation, not classes and portions of it.

The Liberals—there are still Liberals—have old
traditional objections and suspicions; the thin blood
of theoretical republicanism still trickles through a
few veins. But they look around them, at the world
outside, a world chiefly of corruption or anarchy or
cruel despotism; they see that ours is a less illiberal,
a more actively liberal, form of government than any
other open to us. Down at the bottom of their
Radical hearts they are as sensible to the Crown's
emotional and historical appeal as the others.

Then Labour. A survey of all the currents and
cross-currents would be here the most interesting,
and important. It is not possible, for anyone, to make
any such survey; for one reason because this wise
party simply refuses to air its views on the delicate
issue. To the annoyance of the executive, *Is
Republicanism the policy of the Labour Party?* crept one
year on to the public agenda of the Party Conference.
386,000 voted Yes. 3,694,000 voted No.

So baffling, so immoral a result was highly distressing to many leading Socialists abroad. Many of
whom, having the blessings of republican rule, are

now in exile; or gaol; or, tortured and murdered, in their graves.

There are other such baffling indications. Take a foot-rule and measure the space allotted to Jubilee or royal funeral in conservative *Times* and socialist *Daily Herald*. The result may surprise you.

Honourable elements in the party, extremists from the desolate mining counties, who know the horror of the coal villages, the Glasgow slums, the unemployment, underfeeding and despair, the concentrated iniquity of capitalist incompetence and inequality in the regions they come from and speak for, may incline not unnaturally to see the far-away kingship in its setting of West End Society—the King living his personal life in outward ways as one of the rich—as a thing alien, potentially hostile, at best tawdrily irrelevant to the desperate human wrongs to the redress of which they are pledged.

The few actual king-baiters belong almost without exception to less pleasant elements of the party: its smart set, Eton and Winchester out slumming; gentlemen of title, gentlemen not very English; interlopers, ambitious flitters.

I have myself met only one single figure in this Party who wholeheartedly desires the disappearance of the monarchy. "As long as it's there," he said, "we shall never get a Labour Government carrying out a real Labour policy." He meant, I discovered after a while: carrying out a policy like that of the murderous police autocracy of Moscow (a beautiful government, he told me, that he admired from the bottom of his heart). He is a brilliant, and probably even a sincere, man. He is un-English in race and reason and understanding.

There is an egregious couple, husband and wife, who from on high confer advice upon the working classes; a pair better known for their industry than their humour, for their knowledge of blue books than of humanity; he a lord, she of extreme capitalist affiliations. In 'A Constitution' of their own which they have drawn up for us, they graciously decide, after anxiously weighing the pros and cons, that on the whole they will retain the King; warning him, however, that if he wants to keep his job—and gain the approval of magnates' daughters and mushroom peers—he must, taking example no doubt by them, *acquire better manners.*

The great mass of Labour stands on the other side. The Trade Unions, the leaders of working-class origin, the average Englishmen and women. If a little suspicious of its own top men being corrupted by the Court, it refuses to haze the King. However reluctantly, and ragingly, the country-house adherents of the party have to conform, and tie their long tongues a little.

Logically, Labour should be against the fantastic thing. Being English, it is not logical. Wheatley, the extremest member of the first Labour Government, said: I would never lift a finger to change this country from a capitalist monarchy into a capitalist republic. Lansbury, the extremest member of the last Labour Government, said: I have no fear of the Royal Family. Clynes said: The most extreme of our economic doctrines are consistent with the continuance of the monarchy.

These men are not bloody fools. They know they have greater freedom to work for their full programme of social justice and freedom and a better chance of attaining it *than in any republic there has ever been in the world.*

The throne, if hardly the cause of our better state of affairs, is a symptom and guarantee of it. Englishmen who vote Labour know this, not less well than other Englishmen do. Neither on grounds of social justice, which is their goal, nor of mere tactics to reach that goal, have they any intention of calling in question the outward form of our government. "Put the word Republic," said the veteran agitator, "at the head of your programme, and you will spend the next two generations fighting wastefully, hatefully, spilling blood over shadows and symbols, and we shall never get to questions of social welfare at all. You will spend your lives tilting at windmills. And possibly in the end the windmills will defeat you. Make the concession of form on your side and you can get, with infinitely greater ease, the concession of the substance from the other."

Leave it alone.

.   .   .   .   .

The average Englishman desires to.

He takes the Press praise of the royals with a grain, a large grain, of salt. He is quite aware of the king-ship's defects and limitations; in many moods, like Doctor Johnson, he would not give half a guinea to live under one form of government rather than another. He is decided by a few simple considera-tions in favour, not of monarchy in the abstract, but of the British Monarchy in fact.

It is practical, yet with the frills that you need. It is a good piece of machinery; adaptable. It works.

It is stable. It continues on its way without blood-shed or brawl. It is un-corrupt and incorruptible.

It is more interesting than those republics. A king has a greater interest than an elected president —or than no president—in his people, and they in him. We prefer at the top an historic family to a chance politician, a visible man to an abstraction.

It is necessary. Without it we lose the Empire. It is acceptable to every party, and to each loyal Dominion.

Abolish the King, good. What are you going to put in his place?

Who? How?

For the Empire, in what way are four hundred and ninety million people, in hundreds of various terri-tories, going to appoint the new alternative head?

For our home government, either the new President or Protector who would replace our king would become powerful (as the Washington Presidents have become; as Monsieur Millerand, they say, tried to become), in which case it would be at the expense of the Cabinet and Parliament, and of free government as we know it; or, he would *not* be politically powerful, in which case he would only be our king under another name, and with none of our king's advantages.

Any change would be for the worse.

A king will have to provoke us more than any is ever likely to, before we throw overboard the old institution we have always known. It is the longest tradition that any country has. Windsor is the oldest royal palace in the world. We are a sentimental people, and we are attached to it. We are a practical people, and you will have to show us some very solid advantages to be gained before we decide to change the form that has suited us, by and large, for over one thousand years.

We are a grown-up people. We have outgrown dictators and republics. We have had our king-killing, once, long ago. We have had our taste of the saints and the spies and the soldiers.

The King is good enough for us.

Leave him alone.

WHAT
THE
KING
IS

I

THE King is the Living Head of the British nation and empire.

He is the titular political head or Ruler and the effective ceremonial head or Representative Person.

He is, by the Grace of God, of Great Britain, Ireland and of the British Dominions beyond the seas King; Emperor of India; Defender of the Faith.

He holds his title by act of parliament: by the Act of Settlement of the year 1701, which settled the Crown upon the most excellent Princess Sophia, electress and duchess dowager of Hanover, and the heirs of her body being Protestants.

This law, as the books explain, is a law 'like any other.' It has been amended more than once, and in more than one respect, in the past. It may so be amended in the future. It could 'like any other' Act of Parliament, concerning licensing hours or a local gasworks, be repealed totally. To-morrow, at its good pleasure, Parliament could settle the crown upon another family than the Windsors—upon the Macdonalds or the Mosleys, the Crippses or the Churchills—or upon no family, simply abolishing the post.

If he breaks any of the terms of the contract, the King forfeits his crown: if, for example, he ceases to join in communion with the Church of England or marries a Roman Catholic. He may marry a Baptist or a Unitarian, or a Plymouth Sister or a Peculiar Person, or a (female) soldier or sailor in the Salvation Army or Salvation Navy, for all of these are 'Protestants'; but not, without losing his throne, a Papist.

The King, in brief, is a functionary appointed by Parliament; holding his post by Act, and pleasure, of Parliament; dependent, through Parliament, on the will or whim of the nation. He is an employee. He can draw his wage and avoid dismissal only by pleasing his masters and faithfully observing the conditions of his contract. He is a hireling.

He is a god.

The mystical title is stronger, far stronger, than the legal one; if you could compare incomparables.

Lawyers are telling the truth on one plane when they lay it down that the basis of the kingship is statute; and if ever indeed in England the royal office were abolished, it would probably be abolished by, or through the forms of, Parliament. On a different plane of reality, the irrational aspect of the King is his substance, his significance and his strength. The arguments of no lawyers and no philosophers, of no rebels and no rationalizers, no twentieth-century freedom from the power of mystery or superstition (if it had any such freedom), can ever entirely divest the name of *King* or the man who bears it of an ancient magical meaning beyond logic or law.

The first known religion is a belief in the divinity of kings. The first known kings are haloed with the divinity of religion. Sometimes, in the history of some peoples, it is God Himself Who is the king. Saul, David, Solomon are but earthly regents: the true King of Israel is Jehovah. Or the king is the god; as with the Japanese their Mikado, or with the people of Orissa, when they chose as their heavenly goddess Queen Victoria. Or he is son of the god; as Pharaoh was son of the Sun God and of his sister-wife the goddess Isis. Or $\theta\epsilon\hat{\iota}os$, enthroned by the god; as the Homeric kings by Zeus. Or a manifestation of God; as the Incas were Children of the Sun. (He is King of the Forest, he is Lord of the Wood. I'll be the Queen of the May, and you King Whitsuntide.) Or a similitude of the God; as Charles the Martyr of Christ the Paschal Lamb; like whom he died for others, like whom he died at three in the afternoon, like whom he lives in heaven. Or God is *in* him; accurately the Mangaians called their kings god-boxes. Or he is a high priest of the god: as at Sparta, where the kings offered up the State sacrifices; as at Rome the *Rex Sacrorum,* the *Pontifex Maximus;* as in Mexico, their fighting king-priests unto Montezuma at the end; as in Tibet the Dalai Lama.

119

The belief, with all the multitudinous shades that make up the colour of history, is that the High Power which is the mystery of the world, the Unknown God whom the twentieth century after Jesus knows no better than the twentieth century before Him, is in some special way or in some special measure present in the person who symbolizes the high power of that only lesser mystery which is the nation, the tribe, the people. This belief subsists, overlaid however deep by modern habits of reason, or unreason, and is the root of Desire for Kings. It is a belief with which Whigs, radicals, logicians, materialists, plutocrats, Bolsheviks, each with their own strange beliefs or strange absence of beliefs, have still to reckon; with which poor Edward of Windsor himself has to reckon.

The belief in its highest hour gave birth to that theory of the Divine Right of Kings which saved Europe from anarchy, and cruel tyranny of sects, from presbyter and papalist; saved England from the Curia and Scotland (a little) from the Kirk.

The belief still colours to-day our emotional attitude to even the emasculated monarchy of 1937. Twentieth Century works its enlightened will on Victim Edward, advertises, commercializes, publicizes, vulgarizes him; and yet, still, has not been able to put quite out the ancient spark of godhead in his eyes. Nor of belief in it in ours.

Dictators and self-made despots have, as a rule,

higher personal prestige. They lack the true king's prestige, which is priestly; of his office. They lack the prestige of his sacred blood. Some of the marks of monarchy they bear. The greatest thing about Cromwell, that mysterious power in him that by no right of election or public designation made him our Head, was in its elusive nature pure-monarchical; no Parliament chose him, but God or the Devil— like a king. When, however, the living being that is the point of the tribe's unity has also the attribute of legitimate right or historic heredity—when the old word king is his natural name—the awe he inspires is of a deeper quality, and more enduring, than the respect imposed by the representative self-chosen, the ruler raised up by demonic character or military might. Cæsars—Augustus, Napoleon, Mussolini—will be greater men and minds than the average of descended kings. The obedience to them will contain more of devotion to the man and less of loyalty to the office; the force compelling obed-ience will have more of the naked and physical, and less of clothed custom and unconscious consent. The atmosphere will be dynamic not dynastic; it will be less calm, and storms nearer. Hypnotic half-Cæsars—Mohammed, Judas Maccabæus, Hitler— rouse a religious fanaticism in their subjects, who see them as saviours, bearing the sins, the shames, the sufferings of the people.

The milder kings of old right stand in a saner,

because less one-sided, fashion for all the aspirations of their people, both humdrum and high. They are less dramatically deified. The relationship with God is more like an old family connection, acknowledged and comfortably taken for granted by all three parties.

Of the two great types of sovereignty indigenous to Europe, our English monarchy has always partaken more of the Teutonic—kingship pure—than of the Prince of the Roman order. *Imperium*, which the dictators have (but not the other), was in England so to speak tacked on. It is this tribal hereditary element in kingship, usually the milder element, that is truest to the true origins and nature of monarchy. It connects the king, by the most simple and magical of all ties, the tie of blood, with the living past of his people; with the kings and the gods from whom he comes.

As our King comes.

On his slight shoulders Edward VIII bears the weight of the fullest ancestry and the longest continuous tradition in Western monarchy. He is head of the most ancient line of rulers in Europe. With right composite, cumulative, such as few lords of the world have had, he is offspring both of the first English rulers and of those who bore rule here before the English ships came. In his veins runs the blood of one thousand kings. Beyond them, by oldest tradition, the blood of the gods.

Of those who preceded him upon his own throne of England he is sprung from George V; Edward VII; Victoria. From the first three Georges. Among the Stuarts from the first of them, James I; among the Tudors from the first of them, Henry VII; among the House of York from the first of them, Edward IV. From the first three Edwards. From the first three Henrys; with John. From William the Conqueror.

Of kings of Old England, he comes out of Edmund Ironside, Ethelred the Unready, Edgar; Edmund the First, Edward the Elder; Alfred the Great. Out of Ethelwolf; and Egbert, founder of the Wessex House. Beyond Egbert, out of Cerdic, the Saxon chieftain who landed before Year 500 to conquer the isle of Britain and to found, unbeknown, the principal dynasty of history. Beyond Cerdic out of Wotan; called also Woden, Odin; King of Valhalla.

He comes, on other lines, from the old Mercian House and other Heptarchical princes; and, through Queen Alexandra, from Canute.

His right to rule the Celt in us is equal. He is out of Vortigern, Cadwallader, and the chiefs of the Ancient Britons. He is descendant direct of the first independent monarch of North Britain, Kenneth McAlpine, and of the last, Mary Queen of Scots. Beyond Kenneth, and across the Galloway Firth, of earliest High Kings of Erin.

Outside our islands, illustrious forefathers rise up from each ancient throne to claim him. Kings of

France and of Spain, Dukes of Normandy and Anjou, Saxony and Russia. Pedro the Cruel and Saint Louis. Frederick Stupor Mundi; Henry the Lion, Henry the Fowler. Rollo and hosts of wild Vikings. Charlemagne, Wittikind his heathen foeman; Charles Martel, Charles the Bold. He goes unto Emperors of Byzance; east beyond them to Arsacid kings and strange Oriental dynasties. He goes unto David of Judah: the proofs satisfied Queen Victoria. (The proofs of the ancestry, not of the ancestor's morals. Because of his *inexcusable* conduct towards Uriah the Hittite, she announced that she would not permit him to be presented to her even in Paradise.)

Through David unto Jesse, unto Ruth. Unto Jacob, Isaac, Abraham. Noah; Methuselah. Seth; Adam. G O D.

All this, when some chance aberration of England gives to redshirt or blackshirt the momentary mastery and to them the desire to destroy him, all this may not greatly avail him. Or it may.

Head of the State, heir of the ages; parliamentary hireling, god—the King is also a human being.

He is both an institution and a person, a mechanism and a man. There is the Crown, and there is the King. The Crown lies in the Tower; not these many days has a king lain there. No law makes the distinction between the two concepts, and no lawyer can separate them quite satisfactorily. History has

124

institutionalized the king; Nature leaves the institution personified.

Broad differences can be seen. The powers of the British Crown the institution incline always to increase—the armies of civil servants, for instance, who double their numbers with each generation, like rabbits, are the servants of the Crown not of Parliament—while the powers of the British King the person tend, or have at least for generations been tending, to decrease: the obvious feature of our constitutional history through the last three centuries has been the steady restriction of the powers of the person and their transfer to the office.

The Crown is a convenient term covering all the immense executive powers of government: it is the great Leviathan. The King is an individual who retains a minnow's fraction of those powers. The King used to govern England through the fact of his ministers. The ministers now govern it through the fiction of the Crown.

When you hear the word Crown ask yourself always what is meant:—the metaphor kept in the Constitution, the bauble kept in the Tower, or the person kept in the Palace; the man, jewel or post?

The King reigns but does not govern means that the personal king does not rule us but that in his name an institutional king does. *The King never dies* means that, although the mortal holder of the post is taken, the post itself goes marching on. *The King is dead: long live the King!* means, in the mind of a constitutional lawyer, How worthy of prolonged preservation is that office which one occupant has just vacated by demise and another occupant now taken over! *My Government* means my friend Mr. Baldwin's. *Rex versus Smith* means that the Law of the Land, not Edward, has a bone to pick with Mr. S. *His Majesty has been pleased to confer a peerage on* means—on more than one known occasion in recent years has meant —here is a rogue and ruffian who has poured gold into our party war-chest on the clear understanding that we should shew our gratitude by making him one of the hereditary legislators of England; His Majesty's powers so to ennoble him are now vested in us, the Cabinet in office, and although His Majesty thinks the fellow the highwayman we ourselves privately admit him to be, and rather grumbles at his name going through, and though that is a pity as we always like to be agreeable to the Palace if we can, still a debt of honour is a debt of Honour, and so . . . .

The man is more interesting. The institution is more important. The monarchy matters more than the monarch.

In this double nature of the Crown and double meaning of the word lies a good deal of the interest, and not only the legal interest, of the matter. The lawyers give their theory. But the institution being also a human being, other human beings, including

126

constitutional lawyers in their spare time, have and cannot but have an attitude of mind, or heart, towards it which goes beyond the precisions and imprecisions of the text-books. *The King is dead: long live the King!* means probably for no single British subject *only* what it means legally. When the late king died men gave a thought, certainly, to the excellence of the continuing institution and the excellence of its automatic continuing as breath left body; but they thought, also, with respect and regret of GEORGE and with hope and human interest of EDWARD.

There are further complications. Our King of Great Britain, mainly ceremonial but still partly political, is the same person as the several Kings of the British Dominions, ceremonial and theoretical entirely. The King of Canada and the King of Australia and the King of New Zealand and the King of South Africa are the same person as the ancient English King, the descendant of Alfred, Cerdic and Wotan; who is the heir of the Great Mogul also, Father of Mother India. All and each are the institution of the British Crown; and all meet in the body, and soul, of a single living being.

It is a God's burden to bear. And he is only a man.

II

He is a Symbol.

If it be true that his role grows ever weaker politically, while only symbolically stronger, the King of England is not thereby fading away. On the contrary, he is returning to the oldest nature of kingship. In the beginning this had little or nothing to do with sovereignty, power, wealth—as at Babylon, Nineveh, Rome, Byzantium, Versailles, Potsdam, it afterwards acquired all these—but was a figurative and mystical office. The king was not a lord and master, but the representative One which the community felt itself to be; not a man of might who owned and ordered and did, but a man of mystery who simply *was*.

The wheel has come full circle; to that ancient role the King of England is returning.

Queen Victoria, who re-made the monarchy, set its steps back on this way. She was not a very important queen because of anything she did; she was only a fairly important queen for things she did not do; she was a supremely important queen for what she was.

And so her successors. Emblems first, men afterwards.

As such, again, they have various aspects.

A national aspect. Since the Victorian Jubilees,

128

the tendency has been gathering strength for our passionate, if not easily articulate, patriotism to centre in the Crown; as symbol of England, sign and embodiment of our unity, of our pride in race and dominion, our history and our glory. Not all Englishmen feel this. Many are too poor to, and a few too proud. Not all who feel it feel it deeply. But the Crown is the most generally accepted national effigy and rallying-point that we have.

Elsewhere the idol is *La France*, the historic name of the brave and beautiful country itself, made living by the French mind and heart; or the mighty army; or Old Glory. With us, the symbols corresponding count for less. England is a beautiful word, and idea; but the sentiment, however intimate and tender, it arouses—a sentiment which 'Britain' and 'British' cannot arouse—is not a political type of sentiment. The Union Jack is unimportant. The army is nothing. The Church is not a truly national church. Parliament, never beloved of the common people, is now on the down grade. In England it is the King.

He is as good an emblem as the others. A human being of historic lineage and function equals a name, or a war-machine, or a piece of bunting. In times of national emotion we turn to him. We take pleasure in him, delicious pleasure; and if a people can take pleasure in a principal part of their government, it is so far a fortunate people, and a fortunate government. Our Sign unites rather than divides us. Whenever the King rides by, or enters our thoughts or our imagination, he brings out good emotions rather than bad: a sense of fellowship with other Englishmen, neighbourliness, the desire and resolve to pull together. He calls forth the altruistic side of patriotism rather than the aggressive; is a sign of peace rather than of war.

He supplies glory, pride and ceremony: ceremonies the people feel they are taking part in, not merely looking at from outside, or below.

There are psychological aspects.

As the primitive king, so ours fulfils certain fundamental human needs: our need to exteriorize, to project, to play-act. Our interest in the births, deaths, weddings, journeys, joys, sorrows of the House of Windsor is not merely, or mainly, snobbery or idle curiosity; it is not only an intellectual interest in the almost human attributes of an inhuman 'convenient convention' or 'working hypothesis.' It is an expression of our need to have daydreams that are practically unrealizable magically realized; to have our grief and our gladness, our ambitions and our frustrations, dramatized, magnified, sublimated. The royalties do all this for us. They are colossal Compensating Personalities. In the crowd which will look on at the coronation pomp there will be many to feel the clamp and glory of the crown upon their own heads.

"A favourite book of my mother's," writes Mr. H. G. Wells in his Autobiography, "was Mrs. Strickland's *Queens of England*, and she followed the life of Victoria, her acts and utterances, her goings forth and her lyings in, her great sorrow and her other bereavements, with a passionate loyalty. The Queen, also a small woman, was in fact my mother's . . . imaginative consolation for all the restrictions and hardships that her sex, her diminutive size, her motherhood and all the endless difficulties of life, imposed upon her. The dear Queen could command her husband as a subject and wilt the tremendous Mr. Gladstone with awe. How would it feel to be in that position? One would say this. One would do that. I have no doubt about my mother's reveries. In her latter years in a black bonnet and a black silk dress she became curiously suggestive of the supreme widow."

In Mr. Wells's case, his mother's attachment to the Queen drove him the other way. He became jealous of her wealth and power, and of her grandchildren's material advantages. This was no doubt the desirable reaction for a free-born man, and the natural reaction for an assertive one. Would it have been the reaction of the majority of men and women; or even of a majority of men and women, if such there be, on Mr. Wells's own level of brains and understanding?

The King fulfils high joys and ambitions for us:

he bears our sorrows. He also must bear our sins. As of old, he is the Supreme Scapegoat.

We demand a damnably high standard of personal morality from these people. The English king to-day has it as his first duty to behave well, in the Puritan and family sense well; at the very least it is an asset to him if he does so behave, a risk for him if he does not. One who came too far short of the decent middle-class ideal would be in greater danger than for any sort of political errors whatsoever that he might commit.

Victoria and George V, by fulfilling that ideal to perfection, have made it hard for successors of theirs whose natural bent may not lie that way. In a collapsing world, with the old moral values vanishing, the perfect fulfilment of that ideal is the service half the English want from their king.

It is what they feel they are paying him for. And they want their money's worth. A king who didn't give it them they'd bring to heel quickly.

There are cross-currents, of course. In every age there are plenty of subjects who like the king gay; who relish and pardon delights in his life which they might not permit in their own; and who loathe the hypocrisy (which partly it is) of the others. The two hosts do battle over his body; the tribe's two moralities over his soul.

Pleasant for the victim. In the fierce fight all aspects of his soul, and body, are freely exposed.

Such a fight is now, at this hour, proceeding.[1]

If a sovereign otherwise highly acceptable does not, as Edward VII did not, specialize in certain of the virtues specified; then, so long as he does not go, as Edward VII never went, below a respectable and irreducible minimum, the majority (the respectable and irreducible party) averts its loyal eyes and concentrates on the other merits that it requires in a king, and that he does possess—as Edward VII possessed most of them.

Vicarious-virtuous, the King is the country's official exemplar of the virtues. How far example counts in the subjects' actual lives, even when set by a social head with the prestige that the king of the English has, is perhaps debatable. A cynic has surmised that not one single Englishman in Victoria's reign played one rubber of whist the less or put one shilling the less on horses, or had one single lady-friend the less, because his august sovereign so strongly disapproved of cards and racing and adultery. The cynic was probably wrong. At the lowest the Queen's example did something to strengthen tendencies that were there already: tendencies which, by the ancient interplay between prince and people, were already an example to herself. Who influences whom the more is also debatable. It is inextricable. The representative king tends to act as his people

[1] Written end of November, 1936; a matter of hours before the fight became an open one.

133

would have him act; they tend to act, or to desire or pretend to act, as they see him acting.

Whether or no his example is followed, it is at least admired: setting the tone of the hypocrisy, if not the morality, of the age. Even more than it is admired in him, good conduct is required of him. Subjects may do as they like; not so he.

For, as of old, the king is there in the tribe's interest, not his own. He is the nation's arch-servant, to be got rid of if he does not supply the service the nation requires.

His duties now are not rain-making or sun-making, declaring the stars or ruling the River, providing the plentiful crops which those his gifts make possible; but, chiefly, the high personifying of representative qualities—of which the Anglo-Saxon moral standard is one—together with the pure fetishistic duty of *being there*. Whatever the service required, if the king does not give it he goes. The King of the Wood at Nemi, when his power failed him, perished by the hand of his successor; as did Charles I. As long as he seemed to hold good as the sacred taboo of the tribe's prosperity or propriety, they kept him. In the same spirit, projectionary and expiatory, we keep ours.

If he has vices and we yet retain him, these have their use. Upon them, real or imaginary, all the indignation of our own deficient virtue (all the envy of our deficient vice) may royally be wreaked. The wild howl over Tranby Croft and the Prince of Wales's little baccarat game in 1890 was a perfect instance of royalty's scapegoat role. An up-to-date instance is the wrathful whispering, rich righteous whispering, of this present winter of content. We set an inhuman goal for these poor humans; and while the good side in us rejoices if they attain it, the bad side rejoices if they do not. The satisfaction in finding fault with a king is prodigious.

Unctuously we threw upon Kaiser Bill and Little Willie, upon Cecco Beppe and Foxy Ferdie, all the guilt, the guilt of all of us, for the great crime of 1914–18. Our opposite numbers threw it upon Nicholas the Knouter and Edward the War-maker. If there were human beings more guilty of the crime than others, they were officials and journalists and politicians and soldiers and gun-sellers whose unroyal names were not even known to the millions who Aunt-Sally'd the kings.

I was a schoolboy when Princess Ena of Battenberg became Queen of Spain and, to become it, abjured our faith and turned Papist; I remember the news being announced one day at tea-time. "She'll rue it; the woman'll pay dear!" cried a kind man, fanatic deacon-friend of the family's. "Kings and queens are more than us ordinary folks; they know better than others what they're doing. Their sin is greater; they'll pay dearer." He spoke true.

A shocking bomb outrage wrecked the apostate woman's wedding drive, which was a drive of death and blood. "She's *paying!*" exulted the deacon.

It is the obverse side and necessary complement of the adulation. Our own kings, as those foreign ones, may when alive be spoken about and when dead written about with a ferocious freedom not permitted in criticism of any of their subjects; protected, at any rate the rich subjects, by our ferocious English law of libel. Even the written word—though the Press to-day goes very carefully—is freer on the kings. I can write this book about His Majesty the King of England and in it I can say, and I am saying, everything within wide limits of decency that I choose to. But if I were to try to print a bowdlerized particle of the truth about certain powerful *subjects*, even over-night subjects, of His Majesty—if I were to suggest how a certain gentleman, of foreign origin, obtained his tainted peerage; how a certain tentacular family, of foreign origin, acquired the colossal fortune which has assured it its ubiquitous position in our Parliament, Press and public life—I should quickly find myself in a court of law and, two to one, quickly afterwards in gaol.

A famous, the most famous, modern book about Queen Victoria contained a base and baseless aspersion on the private character of Prince Albert. Nothing was done about it; the slander stands, and is no doubt believed by most of the book's readers and relished by many of them. Near the same time appeared another book containing reflections, neither far-fetched nor abnormal—and based, however shakily, on general gossip of the period, gossip which Queen Victoria herself is believed to have believed— on the private character not of her mere Consort but of one of her mighty Ministers. The latter was long dead and was already an historical character. Instantly his descendants, powerful subjects, brought an action against the offending author; who was condemned (it may be quite rightly) and publicly castigated. As the far fouler slander on royalty never was.

King's forfeit corresponds to national character. The Russian Monarchy was a despotism tempered by assassination. The French Monarchy was a despotism tempered by gibes. The British Monarchy is an adulation tempered by moralizing. Righteous and self-righteous criticism, equally with the incense, is showered upon the heads of this our family of crowned whipping-boys and girls. We pay them no doubt for the privilege.

Their good qualities, their tact and courage and dignity, their success in ceremony, are taken ungratefully for granted; but there is an outcry against them for the smallest failing or slip.

Their own worst defect at present is that, alarmed for their pay—for their existence—they the kings bow their heads too low before us the subjects, and take our whippings and carpings lying down; which is not in the part. The other day a member of the Royal Family heard the foulest abuse in her ear ("You — —"), and for answer gave back a smile of royal courtesy; which was unroyally too meek. Themselves are victims of the vacant rationality in the air around them, and doubt their divine role; which is dangerous. They seek to be 'democratic' and, half ashamed, to excuse and whittle away the outrageous pretensions of their office; which are its essence. They behave as though on sufferance, and as though their position could be made to look reasonable; which it cannot. They seek too eagerly to please, are supple and humble and apologetic; which is all quite wrong.

No doubt in every age kings have had their problems of adaptation, and these are merely among their particular problems of to-day. No doubt they are steering a difficult course between opposite currents; between, for example, the desire of most English that royalty should keep its distance, and of many colonials that it should not. No doubt, up to the point where there is no diminution of dignity, a posture of 'democracy' is to-day desirable; perhaps essential. This new King Edward is displaying virtuosity in maintaining the difficult balance between the two, and his own balance on the royal tight-rope.

No doubt, also, they of the present House are aware—as of their special fitness for some aspects of their role—of their unfitness for the extremer part.

For all the new prestige that Victoria and her successors have built up, no one of this line has had the full royal stature, the complete and easy divinity, of their greatest predecessors; has been a person as personally kingly as Henry VIII or Elizabeth or either Charles. They are less royal people to look at. For all their two hundred years upon the throne, they are still not, ideally, the legitimate sovereigns. Robert I and IV will not, except with considerable difficulty, oust Edward VIII; but for the latter, the Usurper, it is more than difficult—it is almost impossible—to assume the divine right of way that belonged to the former's legitimate ancestors. The harm done to our kingship by the 1689 Revolution is still not repaired.

The present family has one special defect of its own, a defect that is almost a virtue: its inaptitude for the things of the mind. The House of Hanover is the least cultivated dynasty of modern history. It cannot represent, as it represents perfectly so much else, the nation's culture and intelligence: except its political intelligence, which matters perhaps the most. Though casting its net fairly wide, it has never included the intellectually creative or curious among those of its subjects whom it has most delighted to honour. These sulk sometimes. It is a pity. They're not very important; but better on the whole to have the *intelligentsia* with you. Meantime, there is no intellectual defence of the throne, which

—Common Sense being inarticulate—is left too much to purveyors of clap-trap, sugar, slush.

The King is there to personify suitably the tribe's manners as well as its morals; to illustrify not only its sexual but also its social standards. He is our Social Head.

He must conform therefore to our ideal of outward modes, and of inward man corresponding to them; to our general national ideal of loving, liking, behaving, thinking, declining to think. He is, and must shew himself, archetype of everything that good-class well-bred people admire and that, in England, most not good-class well-bred people admire equally; looking upwards, humbly, to their betters; beyond them, happily, to the crowned Arche-Better.

Head of this kind of society, he must mirror its kind of taste. In one (unique) word, he must be a Gentleman.

Original kingship knew not that phenomenon. But it held further elements beside the symbolic and the godly-priestly. Sometimes the king was of warrior type, the tribe's *dux* in battle; or a soldier-adventurer who made himself chief of tribes other than his own. The Fighter, the Hero, the Male. These aspects survive in England but slightly, with the unmilitary character of our history and polity. Sometimes he was of patriarchal sort, the head of the tribe his great family. In the sentiment for Victoria, as for George V in his last years, there was something of this: she was the Mother of her people, he Father of a family of nations. (Edward VII the national Uncle: Edward VIII Everyman's Son—or Lover.)

Sometimes the old king was Medicine Man. In England this function died hard. Charles II returned, after a Republic, and during his reign touched 90,000 people for King's Evil. Queen Anne still touched; and Prince Charlie of the true succession, during that ephemeral Court he held at Edinburgh in '45. But George the petty Elector, no royal man at all, clearly to the simplest eye or hope was not able to cure; no subject sought healing at his Hanoverian hands, nor at any of his successors'. Modern ideas, and the less royal personality of the Brunswicks compared to Stuarts or Tudors, have hindered the revival of these powers although the Monarchy as a whole has revived.

The future in such matters is uncertain. With the age's return to mystery, should ever a monarch double the sanctity of his office with a great royal personality of pre-Brunswick stature, he might re-acquire supernatural attributes that would surprise (as they would distress) the materialist-rationalists, almost extinct in so many other fields, who still dominate political science, political sentiment and political prophecy.

Yet finally, in politics also, the King answers to secret requirements of the people. With regard to power, and authority, and control, men have two opposite needs. Men hate to be ruled; they fear and resent restraints on their native (imaginary) freedom. The soul rebels against interference, oppression, suppression; against denial of liberty, denial of liberty of choice. Men love to be ruled; they shirk (imaginary) responsibility, that nightmare of the lonely soul out in eternity, and seek to shift the burden of it on to someone else, both in heaven and on earth. They are frightened of anarchy, the terrible anarchy that may be utter truth of the worlds, and want order in their lives, and their lives to be ordered by Another. They seek a power that will guide and command them, and save their souls from the responsibility and from the anarchy; a power that has right indefeasible so to guide and command them; a liege lord, a fatal Father.

How these two conflicting needs are provided for in the religious sphere, or in the amorous, is not here our theme. In the political sphere, our English system fulfils the two needs by catering for them separately. It supplies a symbolic ruler and a functional ruler. A ruler who is sacrosanct and intangible, giving all the old heroic and mystical sense of lordship; and a ruler who is effective and vulnerable, over whom it is we who have the authority. H.M. and P.M. Edward and Stanley. One is imposed, whatever the

Statute Book says, by divine right of heredity. The other is self-imposed, chosen, by the political device of election.

Chosen so indirectly, indeed, that the choice is not perfectly ours. Mr. Ramsay Macdonald would, it is permissible to presume, scarcely have become the head of any Government of England, Labour or National, if the people of England had had any say whatsoever in the matter; which people, if it could have voted for the other, the hereditary headship, would have chosen King George. By interplay from the other sphere, heredity seems to have played a part in the dazzling fortunes of the ex-Prime Minister's family.

These are but trivial inconsistencies, minor and incidental blemishes in a system that commends itself to us. In the main we find that our admirable constitution gives us, psychologically, most of what we want; combining authority imposed with authority freely self-given, lordship with liberty, magic with common sense.

A system truly admirable from the country's point of view. But from the King's?

That is one grade less certain. That is the one possible catch.

To be modern official and historic ornament, high priest and popular pet, prudent statesman, model of virtue, symbol of everything, physical staring-point

143

and emotional wreaking-point for hundreds and millions of souls, decent chap with quiet gentlemanly tastes and gorgeous fantastic anachronistic idol—one day a man may turn up, a sensitive, a self-conscious, an imaginative man, who will say *No*, I cannot; I cannot fit in all those parts to perfection, to the satisfaction of my intelligence, nor to the peace of my soul.

Lucky for us that, since the job has become what it has become, no such nuisancy man has sat upon the throne. Lucky for him.

III

Our satisfaction with our admirable constitution may be justified. By the facts, and by the future. Our curious compromise, solitary in history, may continue. It may protect us against the ravening public ills of this horrible century.

Such as rage everywhere else. How do those foreigners manage, by the way, who have not this perfect compromise of ours?

The answer is, they manage less well. Whatever, in certain branches, the intellectual or æsthetic or even, though that is unthinkable, the moral superiority of certain other peoples, politically (we feel) all are iller, or at least less well than we.

Their national self-adjustment is less sure. They are less at ease with themselves. Their systems work less well, and they with their systems.

It is a complacent theory; perhaps a true theory.

The poor foreigners, oddly, often hold it themselves. What they think of our kingship might be made an interesting incursion into their psychology, and ours.

The dictator lands rather affect to despise. Their systems offer so much—glory-in-violence, faith, force, triumphant extreme emotion, youth idealism, joy of devotion, joy of hate—that ours does not.

France, who tenaciously disputes with us the world's palm of moral self-sufficiency, is influenced by her view of each individual king of ours' view of *her*. Queen Victoria was supposed to prefer Germany; so, even as she lay dying, was mocked by the Paris newspapers in odious cartoons. Edward VII was known to prefer France, and so was canonized as *notre roi*. When this the prime issue, like or dislike of France, is not prominent, our neighbour can rather admire this curious survival, Majesty; as she admires the Lord Mayor of London, attributing might and influence to both rather beyond anything that either possesses; glad, with a faint note of friendly patronage, to watch the picturesque antics of mediæval ceremony in another country; glad that that country is not her own.

America, of all the other peoples, honours our

throne with the most newspaper space and national attention. There is the patronizing attitude. Poor antiquated king-ridden old England! You can, affirmed Mr. Ambassador Page, have no security in any part of the world where there is government with a king. You cannot, he averred, conceive of a republic that would unprovoked set out on a career of conquest. A king is a mediæval survival, always comic, usually bad. The English are too stupid and too snobbish to abolish theirs. There is a high and enlightened attitude, lofty regret that the other Anglo-Saxon empire should retain a system that is the Negation of Democracy: a system allowing "no scope for a real democracy's free acts of self-expression." (Such for example as burning a poor woman alive, a poor wretched black creature with child, and taking the baby born prematurely in the horrible flames to kick about, till dead, as self-expressive republican football?). There is scorn and hatred, based on a compound of historical grudges, Irish influence, ignorance and an aggressive inferiority-complex: hence the nation-wide enthusiasm for Big Bill Thompson when he threatened, superfluously, to 'drive King George out of Chicago' and, elegantly, to 'bust him on the snout.' There are gibes and sneers at various aspects of our Peculiar Institution; emulating perhaps, although never equalling or indeed hoping to equal, the self-righteous perfection of British sneers and gibes at things, people and institutions American. There is friendly, sometimes half-envious, interest. There is wild snobbery. There is lastly—principally—a wise, wide and decent recognition that our thing is right enough for us; as theirs for them.

Which might, in a word, be the thesis of this book; if it had one.

Other men, other methods—other mummery. For England, the King is the national mystical possession, the necessary form and figment of the State. We are a great people, and ours is a great King.

WHAT
THE
KING
DOES

I

WHAT the King does is less important than what he is.

His occupations are executive and political; representative and ceremonial; private and personal.

The three overlap. Some of his activities partake of both a political and a ceremonial nature, or lie on the border-line between the two. Not much of his so-called private life is devoid, is allowed by his subjects and masters to be devoid, of some measure of public significance.

Which of the Crown's powers are still the King's? What acts may he yet perform on his own initiative, and not as the mere agent or automaton of the Cabinet? Of the might of the mediæval KING, feudal lord of all land and lieges, marching man who led the nation to war, actual administrator who ordered its daily doings in time of peace, what residue remains to this shy twentieth-century civilian called by the same high name? Precisely what does this exalted strange personage, who in political theory is still almost everything, in practice in 1937 politically *do*?

Questions difficult to answer. The King himself could not answer them. If anyone could, it would be a learned constitutional lawyer doubled by a Prime Minister of long experience, clear judgment and in present office: a person who does not happen, never has happened, to exist.

The difficulties are of many kinds.

Between the personal monarch and the institutional monarch the dividing line is shadowy. Under our unwritten and ever-evolving constitution his personal powers are undetermined and indeterminate. They are always changing, in both kind and quantity. We are never up to date in our information. We know how much power each earlier Hanoverian exercised; we know all that can, or need, be known about Queen Victoria's political activity and almost all about Edward VII's. But about George V's very much less, and must await the passage of time and the confidences of the great. Books are always behindhand. Ministers and courtiers are discreet, and the kings themselves discreeter. The only two English kings who held forth about their kingly rights were Scots; a dialectical argumentative couple, father and son, one of whom pedantically sharpened the axe that came down upon the unfortunate head of the other.

The answers would depend on human, as well as political, factors. These are continually changing. On the tone, policy and personnel of the party in power; on the character of the Prime Minister of the moment; on the character of the reigning king; on how long he has reigned. Influence having been substituted for power as the Crown's mode of action, the individual influencing and the individuals influenced are the terms of the equation. These fluctuate.

The lawyers do not let themselves be discouraged by such difficulties. They compile their kingly Cannots—impressive lists of them.

The lists prove, briefly, that the great historic prerogatives of the king are precisely those prerogatives he may not exercise; that the principal things he is supposed to be able to do are the principal things he cannot do. He cannot decide or control the general policy of the country. He cannot publicly express an opinion on matters of State. He cannot choose the Prime Minister, or the other ministers. He cannot dismiss them. He cannot dissolve Parliament. He cannot refuse his assent to a bill. He cannot attend meetings of the Cabinet. He cannot refuse to take the Cabinet's advice. He cannot take advice from persons outside the Cabinet. He cannot exercise his royal prerogative of mercy. He cannot cede territory. He cannot make war, peace, treaties, peers, bishops, judges. The king can make speeches, but not the King's Speech.

Some of these absolutes are doubtful.

The King can still influence policy. He can confidentially press a policy upon his Prime Minister, seek to dissuade him from another, delay the execution of a third. George V required that second general election before he would give his consent to the creation of the Parliament Bill peers. If there is no single clear instance of any of Victoria's governments, still less a government of any of her successors, changing an important item in their programme to suit the monarch's personal taste, yet the Queen was not powerless. She was a permanent brake on (spoke in the wheel of) half her ministries. The Liberal ones.

When the party called to power has no undisputed leader, the King still has a say in choosing the Prime Minister. Victoria sent for Rosebery in preference to Harcourt. George V had a word in the selection of Baldwin in preference to Curzon; perhaps a big word in the replacement of Ramsay Labour by Ramsay National.

He has not quite lost the power of appointing, or at least successfully suggesting to the Prime Minister, individual members of the Cabinet. Balfour brought in some ministers on Edward VII's recommendation, Campbell-Bannerman at least one minister. How far, since then, the King has had a hand in Cabinet-making is not accurately known. As late as Edward VII he was believed to be influential, if he desired to be, in the choice of the Foreign Minister and the War Minister in particular.

His prerogative of dissolution is not obsolete.

The Cabinet decides to dissolve Parliament, but it must get the King's consent. This is not always a formality, and a situation is possible in which he might refuse it; or in which, in consultation with the Prime Minister, his judgment one way or the other might be decisive. Whether or no he may decide a dissolution, he can certainly refuse one.—Can; but scarcely *will*. In all that touches the Parliament, the theoretical possibilities of the 1937 King's powers are different from the practical probabilities. Over against the Commons, and as regards power over them, it is the Prime Minister who has taken the old place of the King. (Who has taken the Prime Minister's? . . .)

His veto is dead; but he can still get small changes made in a bill.

He can, in a crisis, see leaders of the Opposition and in a measure mediate between them and the Government. As King George saw Lord Lansdowne at the height of Peers versus People.

If, happily for himself, the sovereign no longer exercises the prerogative of mercy, thus escaping the hysterical attacks that fall upon the Home Office when the noose nears the neck of some popular murderer, his personal view, if he has one, is said to carry weight with the Home Secretary. Edward VII had ideas of his own about Lynch the Irish 'traitor' who fought for the Boers; about Edalji the Parsee lawyer accused of the Wyrley horse-maiming; about

155

Raynor the murderer, and maybe son, of William
Whiteley the Universal Provider. In at least one of
those three cases his views had effect on the outcome. And did not the Queen-Empress succeed,
or almost, in saving the Senapati of Manipur?

In the King's Speech the King can suggest changes
of word, and nuance. These changes the Prime
Minister may refuse to make, but is believed more
often to accept.

The King can object to names in the Honours lists,
and the Premier will sometimes bow to the royal
distaste. He secures a modest place for friends and
nominees of his own; in special lists, such as Jubilee
and Coronation ones, quite a large place if he likes.
If he tries to make it too large, or to fill it too
quaintly, even at those special times of royal privilege
there may be trouble. It is said that the tolerant
Salisbury (who might have been more tolerant,
remembering his own Alfred Austin) could not quite
stomach the gorgeous non-Aryan complexion of
Edward VII's would-be roll of honour in 1902; and
jibbed. It is said, though not in the books, that the
ensuing row was the cause of the old Premier's
resignation.

To the Royal Victorian Order in fact, and to the
Order of Merit somewhat more than in theory, the
King appoints personally.

Some ambassadors are appointed, or sent to this
post instead of that, on the royal suggestion; and

some dismissed. Victoria removed at least two.

In nomination to certain great offices of state the King's preferences can prevail, particularly as regards bishops and the colonial governors. Against Lord Salisbury's choice Edward VII was able to force through his own, probably better, candidate for the see of London; still its occupant. *He* jibbed at the appointment of Alfred Austin, an obscure political hack of Salisbury's, as Poet Laureate; "because," he said, thus showing that his taste was not so bad after all, "of the trash the fellow writes," and of which he sent the noble marquess a large package of choice samples. He finally gave in, and grumblingly accepted the wretched poetaster:—"as long as he gets no pay."

There are posts to which the King has re-acquired in our own time the right of appointment. Such are the great offices of the Household: the Lord Chamberlain, the Master of the Horse, the Lord Steward. Until 1924 these offices changed hands with each new government. The Government of that day—the first Socialist Government of England—decided, with a curious mixture of deference and indifference, that they need change hands no longer.

Even were they accurate, the lawyers' negatives would be accurate for a shifting instant only. At times, each different but none very distant, the King could do all the forbidden things in their list.

Historians fix the date when this or that power was

exercised for the last time. No sovereign since Queen Anne has vetoed a single bill; none since Queen Elizabeth has vetoed more than one or two bills: she quashed forty-eight. None since Anne has attended a meeting of the Cabinet. None has been the real ruler of the country since William III, or decided main lines of national policy since George III. As late as George IV the king could really choose the Prime Minister. As late as 1885 there was a chance of a government that enjoyed the support of Parliament going out because it lacked the support of the Queen (and perhaps of the nation); but Gladstone could survive even Gordon. As late as 1893 a queen could secure a pointed change in a Queen's Speech: from Gladstone's reference to a bill for the better government of Ireland she forced him to delete the 'better.'

Yet no one can say that the last time a prerogative was exercised was the last time—will be the last time —it could have been exercised. The decline in the royal power is evident; but no one can be sure that the decline will continue, or that a reverse process may not set in; may not now be setting in. There are signs pointing both ways.

All that is sure and certain is the fact (regretted by some, approved by others) that, as long as there is a person in the State called *King,* some measure of influence and therefore power he must continue to possess. He can never become the pure rubber stamp of Whig desire. He will always know many people, see many people, hear many views, have access to many papers; always be a man as well as a mechanism.

Throughout the most depressed period of the royal power, from, say, the death of the Prince Consort to the middle years of George V, the sovereign has continued to be something more than a cipher. The titular ruler's objections, suggestions, proposals for the modification of a measure or a policy have, in even the lowest hour, been listened to with respect by the political ruler; and, added Asquith, with greater respect than suggestions from any other quarter whatsoever. He bears the glamorous name of King.

If he is ordinarily wise, when he has been on the throne during a few ministries he will have joined experience to glamour. Ministers come and go; he stays. His time averages four times as long as theirs; he can become four times as experienced. Victoria had ten Prime Ministers, and saw some twenty changes of government. No Prime Minister of hers was ever in power for more than six years at a stretch; she was in power unbrokenly for sixty-four. She looked upon them as the inexperienced, and the ephemeral, part of government. They were temporary officers in the regiment; she was on sentry duty for ever.

The King of England has almost no power left for evil: a good deal for good.

The last prerogative may go. No man called King will ever be without at least some residue of at least informal rights. Even if they are but the old trio, as valid as in Bagehot's day, and as valuable: the right to be consulted, the right to encourage, the right to warn.

The King can warn. In effect he says: 'Well, my dear Mr. Baldwin, you are the responsible man; I am not. Go forward with this matter if you wish to; if you must. It's your funeral, not mine. But remember this precedent; don't forget what happened on that occasion. Really I should hardly do it if *I* were you.'

The King can encourage. His 'I am with you' gives a Ministry heart, and added assurance that their policy is wise to pursue.

The King must be consulted. In other climes and times it has been the chief privilege of a prime minister to have the right of access to his king: our king, Looking-Glass fashion, has as his Gilbertian chief privilege the right of access to his prime minister. He has the right to see him and to say what he thinks or likes on whatever he is told. Before a Cabinet meeting at which big decisions may be taken the two meet and talk the matter over, and the Prime Minister hears the King's views. He need not adopt them. Possibly he sometimes does. How often is not known. There is no means of finding out.

Quite separate now is the sovereign's work as king

—kings—of the Dominions. Imperial business takes every year a larger place in the royal time-table.

The Governors-General now representing not the Government of Great Britain nor the London Parliament but the King alone, he is in direct touch with them without any intervention of the home Cabinet. Free of the Prime Minister of England, he transacts regular business with the Dominion High Commissioners.

Of the gathering prestige of, and the new duties devolving upon, the Royal Family through its imperial role, two recent decisions afford, by their contrast, curious evidence. As late as 1928, the Council of State set up to perform the royal duties during King George's first illness included the Prime Minister and the Lord High Chancellor of England. But, in 1936, the Council of State appointed for King George's last illness included members of the Royal Family only. It was felt no longer suitable to include any subjects; who would have been subjects of one of the King's countries, Great Britain, alone.

II

Whatever the precise position of the prerogatives and the present measure of the King's political powers may be—and it is quite unimportant—the exercise of these remains a considerable portion of What He Does, and takes up a considerable proportion of his *time*.

Of the Prime Minister's time also; which a Prime Minister with a less lofty idea of the king's office than of his own—Balfour, perhaps, or Lloyd George—inclines to regard as so much time wasted. Some of Victoria's Liberal Governments did have to expend rather a large part of their energies in quarrelling with the Court. "The Queen alone," groaned Mr. Gladstone, "is enough to kill any man."

How does the King perform his business of State?

In the first place by oral communication, interviews with—audiences granted to—his Prime Minister and the other ministers.

Queen Victoria, of course, worked chiefly by correspondence, that famous correspondence, the most interesting in royal records; and wrote, and underlined, more words than any other monarch in the history of the world.

The Queen is surprised. She is astonished, amazed, vexed, grieved, grieved to add, alarmed, *much* alarmed, shocked, *dreadfully* shocked, shocked *beyond measure;* furious, *quite* furious. She finds things—many things—not suitable, not creditable, unwise, dangerous, indecorous, factious, unpatriotic, sad, lamentable, astounding, dishonest, impertinent, insolent, shameful, disgraceful, abominable, scandalous, monstrous, disrespectful, *most* disrespectful, incomprehensible, *utterly* incomprehensible. She feels strongly, she cannot but think that, she must not leave unnoted the fact that, she feels deep pain that, she cannot refrain from expressing her surprise (alarm, indignation) that, she has no alternative but to, she most emphatically declines to, she feels *most strongly*. Mr. Gladstone *must*. Mr. Gladstone must *not*. It is atrocious of Mr. Gladstone. This incredible Government. They have behaved atrociously, infamously. The Queen will not swallow this affront. *Very* peculiar and objectionable. *Most* curious. *So* provoking. Too, *too* dreadful. On no account should moustaches be allowed without beards; *that* must be clearly understood. . . .

One can snigger, as the nineteen-twenties did. One can moralize, or politicize. One can see in her a narrow, violent, pugnacious, obstinate, shrewish old lady, hindrance not help to her ministers, little fat mountain of prejudice, formidable engine of glorified partisan obstruction, holy terror to all around her. Yet those multitudinous letters are among the most sincere, vivid and readable ever written; and the reader's gathering and finally prevailing impression, as he follows the unflagging pen, must be of the industry, the integrity, the zeal, the zest, the common sense, the shrewdness, the knowledge, the understanding, the unique sincerity; the never surpassed realization of a role and devotion to the duties it imposed.

Ministers to whom the letters were addressed may sometimes have judged them less favourably. For they were inexorable; they were perpetual. Her authority had to be sought, and the Minister's reasons set forth at length and in writing, before any important step could be taken. The principal foreign despatches were written about line by line. It was irritating for the Minister, who regarded himself as the true sovereign; but there it was. There She was.

The staying and delaying that Victoria's existence involved was probably, in the great majority of cases, a good thing. A Prime Minister could bully his colleagues; he had to think out, and carefully and patiently and politely explain, the reason for his proposed action to the one person in the world who could, and did, bully *him*. It was probably a good thing. It made for clarity and, in foreign affairs, for safety.

Edward VII, no penman, did not shew the same exclusive preference for his mother's method. He used, each in reasonable measure, the pen, the personal audience, the telephone and that increasingly important and hard-worked official and go-between, the royal Private Secretary. Letters to Edward VII from the Prime Minister, the Foreign Secretary, or the Minister for War were still always in their own hand. He wrote on them 'Appd. E.R.,' or 'Seen E.R.' If he disagreed, or had suggestions to make, he jotted down his views, which the Private Secretary re-drafted—possibly bowdlerized—and sent back to the Minister.

George V's Prime Ministers, apparently, did not either see or write to him fully on most questions. One or two of them treated him to the extent they dared, and that was possible, as the figure-head, Duke of Venice, or rubber stamp of their ideal. But in Parliament Bill days, and around the outbreak of the War, Asquith and his king were in continuous communication, oral and written. And at the end of the reign, when George had a firmer hand on things, audiences became more frequent again and the correspondence more important.

The King has business to transact with other principal men in the State besides the Cabinet ministers:—with Officers of the Household, officers of the army and navy, ambassadors, prelates; with high officials of the government departments.

Affairs and the world grow ever more complicated. The King's, like the Prime Minister's, familiarity with each separate department must inevitably grow less, and be confined to proportionately fewer aspects. Take the Foreign Office. George V's relation with this, the most august, the most traditionally royal Department of State, seems to have been confined to the following. He saw some despatches, and perhaps most of the very important ones; occasionally he suggested a change. All appointments of ambassadors, ministers and counsellors (though not of even the highest Foreign Office officials) were submitted to him. The submissions were pretty well formal, except that for a few particular nominations, for example to the Scandinavian Courts where the Royal Family has kinship, His Majesty's pleasure was genuinely taken. Proposals for orders and decorations went to the Palace always. In addition to the Secretary of State, the King occasionally received the highest officials. —This no doubt was less than his father had had to do with that particular department; George, unlike Edward, was not more interested in the Foreign Office, or in the War Office, than in the other ministries. The ruler of the greatest empire in history never once set foot in his Department of War during the greatest war in history.

His work, of course, is done mainly at the Palace. There he gives audience; there he reads the innumerable papers of all sorts that he still must read; there he finds time, as best he may, to reflect about what he hears and reads.

Much mere signing is still a royal burden: glorified clerical work. There is less of it than there was. If the Royal Sign Manual is still required for the most important executive acts, of more trivial papers the sovereign's pen has gradually been relieved. Queen Victoria signed over 60,000 documents a year; George V not a hundred a day.

The King no longer signs all officers' commissions

with his own tired hand. Victoria was once sixteen thousand commissions in arrears, and used to sit up far into the night to work them off: many officers used to receive their promotion warrants after they had left the army. The Great Queen is the most unliterary person in history who suffered from writer's cramp.

The importance of what he Is gaining continuously upon the importance of what he Does, a 1937 king who immersed himself in papers as deeply as Victoria would scarcely be doing his duty. It would leave him no time for far more necessary duties.

The Private Secretary has for a generation or two been growing in importance, and his staff in size. This royal secretariat, unadvertised and un-self-advertising, includes some exceedingly able men and is said to be the most competent department in London. Only with its help is the King able to cope with his ever-increasing duties. The secretaries map out his day for him, and his year; arrange for his visitors to the Palace, his journeys away from it and all the rest, with an economy of time and a pro-digality of tact adapted to the multifarious persons and occasions. They help him to avoid mistakes; which with five hundred million subjects, each regarding the King as there for him or her, could be made in hourly abundance.

Once in a blue moon they make mistakes them-

selves; as when the State of Kansas, U.S.A., in reply
to a message of condolence on the death of Queen
Victoria, received in the new King's name his heartfelt thanks for their "loyal" message. Kansas rose in
republican dudgeon, which Edward by a tactful
personal letter was able to calm down. The offending
secretary had imagined, presumably, that the strange
name pertained to some minor possession of the
Crown; one of those funny African protectorates or
Pacific islands, don't you know.

They keep voluminous dossiers. They keep
up to date, and the King informed, on every conceivable matter that might touch him. Through
them he knows curiously well what England is doing
and thinking; better, some say, than the Prime
Minister. Their sources of working-class opinion
are laughed at by a few (West End) Socialists, who
allege, no doubt quite inaccurately, that the Private
Secretary seeks it in West End clubs. They keep a
great map of Britain, marked to shew regions
favoured by a royal visit, and when so favoured; and
inform His Majesty when bare places on the map need
filling in. Then, from among the hundreds of
humble requests for the Presence that pour in hourly,
those from Leeds or Leicestershire or Ludlow or
Lossiemouth or whichever the Neglected Areas may
happen to be, are honoured and granted; and an
early progress thither arranged for.

III

Apart from powers, the King retains certain minor *privileges*.

He cannot be had up, or arrested, or put in gaol. His goods cannot be distrained upon, and the police may not raid the Palace. His official income is exempt from taxation, the theory still being that all the revenues of the realm are his and that he cannot therefore tax himself. He pays no rates on his royal residences, and no probate on property he inherits. He cannot be sued for debt or damages; if he declines to pay, there is no legal remedy. (Practice is different from theory: when Queen Victoria's yacht ran down another yacht and three of the crew were drowned, although she was not legally liable she compensated the yacht-owner and the families of the victims with exceptional liberality.) Officers of the Household and royal servants are exempt from services on juries, and privileged from arrest in civil actions. The King has a right to the title Majesty, to a royal salute, to the use of the royal standard. He has a right to every whale caught in territorial waters; the King gets the head and the Queen the tail. His motor-cars bear no registration number, and are not bound by the speed-limit. His telegrams and letters go free; he has no use, except as a collector, for the stamps which bear

169   M

his image. His will and testament is the only one not lodged at Somerset House. Queen Victoria declined to lodge the Prince Consort's will also. Legally perhaps she was in the wrong; it was a nice point.

Apart from these legal privileges, the King has some moral and some practical ones. Heaps of money, splendid houses to live in, freedom from material care. Fear of the financial morrow, the daily fear of three-fourths of his subjects, he is delivered from.

Specific *disadvantages*, on the other hand, attach to his office. He is debarred from giving evidence in a law-case in which he is a party. He may not rent a house or a property, but must buy it outright. He alone in England may take no part in the open game of politics, by speaking, canvassing, voting; although President Lebrun, Chancellor Hitler and the heads of most of the non-monarchical States have a vote, and although a century or two ago his predecessors might, and did, speak and canvass hard. George III was an assiduous party worker, but not George V. *He* could not shamble round the Windsor shops crying "The Queen wants a gown, a gown— No Keppel!"; "The Queen wants a chest of tea, wants a chest of tea—No Keppel! No Keppel!"

In many ways no man in England, except a slave of extreme poverty, is so unfree. He may not choose his destiny, as a duke's or a cook's son may—become

a boxer, sailor, novelist, parson—nor escape it.
He has little liberty for a purely private life, less in
the ordering of his days, none from publicity.

Endless antics and functions, which other men
could evade by changing their job, are the measure of
his days. He can never see life and its shows as his
free subjects see them: he appears upon an ordinary
scene, and at once it ceases to be ordinary. He
cannot stroll along the Strand, or up and down the
front at Blackpool, to enjoy the normal pleasures of
either. Each time he visited the Wembley Exhibition
George V was more or less molested, if only once
objectionably. Queen Victoria supplied a curious
instance of royal unfamiliarity with everyday things
when, after eighty years in the world, she remarked
that she had never seen a railway ticket; it was, she
supposed, a thin sheet of paper? No theatre the
King attends, no train he travels in, is ever quite like
an ordinary theatre or train such as his subjects know;
with privacy, with normality, without fuss. Everything and everybody is abnormal. Bowing never
ceases. Contrary to a general notion, however, the
King has the privilege of *paying* for the royal box and
the royal train.

It is, very likely, the most difficult post in the
world. Hitler and Mussolini move in greater danger;
but their jobs are in compensation more exciting,
media for self-expression which they themselves
have chosen. The President of the United States is

there for four years only: our king's is a life sentence. The Pope is usually an old man when the Holy Ghost elects him, and has only a few years of it to face; like the Mikado, he is largely withdrawn from the public gaze; his personality matters less, and is less exhaustingly worn.

In all ages the prince has found friendship difficult. Those who offer it to him will, however deep down, be at least partly actuated by vanity, or ambition; the hope of rewards, palpable or impalpable; snob's delight. Those who might have pure friendship for him in their hearts are not those who would push forward to offer it. An equal, loving and wholly disinterested friend such as most other men may hope, once or twice in their lives, to be given is beyond a king's common expectation. George V, a very simple and unself-conscious man, had one or two.

In all these intimate ways the political ruler, the Prime Minister, is far better off. There are friends he had before he became Prime Minister; and before anyone knew he would become Prime Minister. While *he* has most of the power it is the king, the Representative Person, who suffers most of the inconveniences and runs most of the dangers.

He is inundated with letters from lunatics, cranks, theorists, horoscopists, magicians, moralists; people with views, people with visions, people with grievances; people who love him, people who hate him; people who threaten to kill him. The impudent intrude upon his scant privacy to gloat over his face. For years, until they were stopped, the Transatlantic tourists who used to crowd into Crathie Parish Church were a torture to King George and Queen Mary, on whose lips and hands even in the act of prayer they republicanly feasted.

Madmen and fanatics are after his person; Humbert of Italy said that the principal duty of a king was to be shot at. When the cruel dagger of 1897 just missed its mark and the blade, cutting through his sleeve, stuck in the upholstery of the carriage, "These are the little perquisites of our trade," he said gamely, pocketing the dagger. Where Acciarito and others had failed, Bresci succeeded in the end.

Our kings run less risk than most of the others; but there were six separate attempts on the life of Queen Victoria.

IV

There are, the second great division of his work, the things the King does because of what he is. All the formal, and representative, and ceremonial, duties of the Crown. The rites of the nation.

He opens Parliament. He holds Privy Councils. He receives Ministers when they come to kiss hands on taking office and when they resign. He receives foreign rulers and pays them visits in their own lands.

He holds Courts and levees. He gives State dinners, semi-State receptions and less formal teas and garden parties. He receives foreign ambassadors and his own, representatives of the Dominions, Indian princes, native chiefs and innumerable other persons and groups of persons, subjects or foreigners, eminent by their station, meritorious by their achievement, or assiduous by their nature: generals and admirals; prelates and proconsuls; nurses, teachers, social workers and trade union leaders; aviators, Australian cricketers, delegates to international conferences, mayors, philanthropists, inventors, scientists, journalists, heroes. Apart from innumerable collective receptions and audiences, and in addition to his continual interviews with ministers, officials and secretaries, he receives over five hundred people a year in individual audience. He confers knighthoods and decorations, affixes medals for saving life and for taking it. He inspects the Fleet, regiments and Air Force, presents colours, and figures in other military, naval and aerial ceremonies. He opens international congresses. He replies—through the Home Secretary, but his answer is often personal—to addresses and petitions from his subjects. He plays the chief part in great national ceremonies of every kind, makes royal progresses in State or semi-State to different parts of his kingdom or empire, rides in cavalcades and processions, attends sporting events such as Test Matches, the Cup Final, Ascot and the Derby; and charity performances and tournaments, and tilts and shows. He inaugurates or visits hospitals, exhibitions, fairs, institutes, museums, schools, bridges, docks, power stations, parks, arsenals, ships, factories, mines; lays thousands of tons of foundation stones; unveils mountains of memorials. He lightens the scenes of disasters by his royal presence or sympathy. He is the nation's and empire's Chief Patron and Chief Almoner, taking the lead in works of charity and in patronage of all major public activities that are non-political. He subscribes heavily to many of them out of his own purse.

Some of these are essential, and many of them can be looked upon as useful, activities. Somebody must perform them. The fact that Majesty performs them adds significance, solemnity or éclat to the events; delights or placates the persons received or honoured; aids all the good causes, encourages the people who are directly concerned in them, and arouses the interest and opens the purses of others. Royalty gives impetus to every cause. In the sun of Majesty's favour things go with more of a swing. You feel your job honoured, and do it better.

Of the ceremonies, some are the most brilliant left in the world, the Pope of Rome alone competing: the pomp and ritual of the opening of Parliament; the glittering scene in the Throne Room at a Court; a State banquet at the Castle, with the Beefeaters in lines, the gold plate, the diamonds, the historic and majestic setting; the unique Coronation—and for us, the mob, admitted to none of these, gorgeous progresses and processions that suffice us.

Whether Majesty itself enjoys the shows will depend on temperament. Victoria was not partial to them. Her son enjoyed every moment of them. His son played the chief part in them so successfully that we never asked ourselves whether he was enjoying himself or not; one took his doing his duty for granted. His son, again, is said not to take great pleasure in the ceremonial side.

It must sometimes be tedious; even though the technique of royalty in suffering bores and chores gladly is exceedingly highly developed.

> *What infinite heart's-ease must kings neglect*
> *That private men enjoy! And what have kings*
> *That private have not too—save ceremony,*
> *Save general ceremony?*

The dullest of deputations must be received with an alert smile; each individual bore given a handshake and a sentence or two of appropriate and interested comment, and sent away happy, and hot royalist. The King will usually have been coached in the subject by one of his secretaries; even so, the proportion of sense he talks is surprising. Memory and quick assimilation of a subject are of course chief objectives of his training. Uncle Bertie and nephew Willie, so unlike in most ways, were alike in their genius for the successful superficiality their jobs required of them.

All day long he has to be changing clothes and uniforms; adapting himself to different aspects of Is, performing variant feats of Does. All day long he has to be gracious and smiling; at the end of the day, dead tired, half dazed perhaps, he must not shew it.

'Tribulation and royalty and patience.'

The division between ceremonial and political is not clearly drawn. Edward VII's State visits abroad, for instance, which were they? Were they figuration or were they high politics?

Leaving aside the controversial aspects of those famous jaunts, which are many—whether they were of great use, or of no use, or worse; how far the whole Entente policy was Edward's own, and how far his ministers'; whether he was himself his own Foreign Minister initiating the policy, or the obedient constitutional servant of Lansdowne and Grey with no opinions of his own; how far the policy was a good policy or a bad policy, a policy that consolidated peace or jeopardized it, the policy that postponed and nearly prevented the War or that promoted it and made it inevitable; whether the encircling of Germany was his aim, or not his aim; whether it was a patriotic and desirable aim or a criminal aim; whether the unsatisfactory human relation between King and Kaiser was more the one's fault or the other's; whether it had an unsatisfactory influence on the relations of their two countries; whether England or Germany (or France or Russia) was more to blame for the outcome; whether his reputation as a diplomatist was deserved, and whether it was a good reputation or a bad; whether, as his eulogists and obituarists declared, he was Edward the Peacemaker or, as the Kaiser saw it, Edward the Mischief-Maker—whatever the truth of all such matters (tremendous matters, bound up with the ruin of the world), Edward's position, abilities and character were such that the part he played on even the most formal of his trips inevitably became political as well as formal.

Whoever contrived the *Entente*—Germany when she rejected England's approaches towards an alliance, brandished her glittering sword and went down to the sea in ships; France bent on *revanche*, or seeking to protect her fair land against a new desolation, protecting her very life; England seeing that the day of proud isolation was over and that she had, or imagined she had, an enemy and so needed a friend; Lansdowne or Edward or Wilhelm; God or the Devil—it was King Edward VII who made it an Entente *Cordiale*.

On the first day of that famous state visit to Paris in 1903, sharp hostile cries of *"Vive les Boers!"* and *"Vive Fachoda!"* greeted his ears as he rode in procession along the boulevards. His suite was booed.

"The French don't like us," complained one of them.
"Why should they?" rejoined the King. When, in the
sullen crowds, anyone chanced to raise his hat,
Edward returned a military salute at once correct
and very cordial.

The first difficult drive over, passably well, he set
to and spent the two or three days that followed in
a supreme and supremely successful effort of tact and
courtesy, and appeal to Parisian sentiment; and when,
on the last day, he rode in procession again along the
boulevards, the one cry heard, sincere and enthusiastic, was *"Vive le Roi!"*

And so, even if he had nothing to do with framing
the policy that sent him to Paris, he had everything
to do with making it a success. Ceremonies with a
capable king in them become more than ceremonies.

Last week, as I write, provides a new border-line
instance. The grandson's jaunt, to Glamorgan and
Monmouth: which was it? Is or Does? Was
Edward VIII merely expressing the 'representative
concern' of the whole country at the plight of one
part of it: or was he getting a move on?

We don't know.

Baldwin may. It is in any case rather in their
King's glory, and in his goodness of heart, than in his
power that those poor men and women place their hope.

Between all these multifarious tasks of the one kind
and the other kind, the King is a hard-worked man.

He keeps abreast by obedience to his doctors, by adherence to a fairly rigid time-table, and with the help of the devoted Private Secretaries. Plan as they may, and the King with them, the twenty-four-hours day and twelve-months year is their chief difficulty and his.

George V stretched both to the utmost. He was up by seven. Before breakfast, sometimes a ride in the Park but always a first hour or two's attack on his correspondence. During breakfast, served at nine-thirty, the newspapers. From ten till noon in his 'office'; documents, secretaries, studying, annotating, signing. Audiences from twelve till one. After luncheon—sometimes a family affair, some-times a function—ceremonies abroad, selections from the list we gave just now. Back to the Palace for two or three hours' more office or more audiences, until dinner: with official guests again very likely. In the evening, bridge or a book sometimes; but often Courts or receptions or parties, or more papers and more audiences until bedtime (ten-thirty) and release.

At Sandringham or Balmoral the chances of rest and amusement were better. On the other hand, more time taken up by the management of the royal estates, financial affairs, social duties.

Edward VIII's time-table is different in several details from his father's; but as full. As dull.

Last of all, the King's own private life remains.

Little of it remains. Of an individual existence free
and unwatched, following his own bent and bearings,
his time and body and soul his own, very little indeed
remains.

Leave it to him.

ALL
THE
OTHER
EDWARDS

IT is a pleasant, and perhaps a profitable, minor circumstance of monarchy that the ruler's name, unlike the names of the dictators and the presidents, calls back for the ruled their country's history —in our English case, and the Edwardian instance, over one thousand years of history.

One thousand and six-and-thirty years ago, in the year nine hundred and one, EDWARD THE ELDER became king of the Angles and Saxons.

He was son of Alfred the Great; he is ancestor of Edward the Eighth. He waged war against the invading Northmen and fought, and won, many tremendous battles. With the help of his Amazon sister the Lady of the Mercians, he subjugated the Danelaw, that great stretch of the east and middle lands which the invaders held. Adding Mercia to his original realm of Wessex, he made himself effective king of England up to the Humber and won a first word of regnal recognition from turbulent Scotland, which "chose him to father and lord." He could read, and probably write. He was brave. He had three wives and fourteen children.

EDWARD THE MARTYR was his great-grandson; the son of King Edgar and of Ethelfled the Duck; the boy Dunstan crowned and coddled.

Not much is known of him except his surname: a possibly misleading surname, since the poor young king was done to death not for his creed by persecutors but for his crown by a stepmother. That lady, desiring to place the latter on her own little boy Ethelred's head, had little King Edward murdered; had him stabbed while astride his horse, from which he tumbled dying, and they dragged him through the woods till he was dead. The cruel deed was disavowed by its beneficiary, Ethelred the Unready, whose mother in revenge thrashed him with a huge wax taper; is called by the old chronicler the worst deed in the history of the Angles since they came to Britain; and was done at Corfe, in Dorsetshire. Little Edward was buried at Wareham, in the same county. He was a pious youth, popular; unmarried, unimportant.

His step-nephew, EDWARD THE CONFESSOR, comes third and last of the pre-Conquest Edwards.

He was fond of fasts and almsgiving, and monks, and Mass. He founded Westminster Abbey. He instituted the miracle of the Royal Touch. He took the vow of chastity. This was hard on the Queen; hard on the chances of the old English monarchy also, and St. Edward's childlessness was a chief factor in the troubles that led to the Norman Conquest. He was too fond of the French. The great Earl Godwin, with whom and his son Harold he was in perpetual bloody discord, seems to have stood for the national sentiment (for what it then was) much more than he the king did. After the Conquest, however, this same national sentiment placed round the Confessor's head a halo of glory and pathos as last of the old English line. "O good Lord!" laments the Golden Legend, "What joy and gladness was then in England!" At each later Coronation the people demanded that "good King Edward's laws" should be observed. At the coming Coronation it is Saint Edward's crown, chair, mantle, tunic that Eighth Edward will use.

Though he would have made an excellent if slightly spiteful saint, the Confessor was no use at all as king. The country was not governed; instead of the king, strife and faction reigned. Englishmen were on the down grade during his reign, in several ways, and probably needed to be conquered.

St. Edward is a shadowy shape. A wan creature, weak and feckless. A namby-pamby nullity. In looks a strange contrast: the tall form, powerful build, golden hair and blue eyes of his Saxon forebears clashing queerly with his priestly pale face and 'transparent womanly hands.' A Valhalla warrior turned virgin, monk and albino.

He was already dying when the Norman threat came near, too ill to be present at the great festival of dedication of his new Abbey of Westminster. A few days later he died, Twelfth Night of 1066; and was buried in his Abbey, at dawn on the morrow. His death-bed sayings are many. Within the year William the Bastard had conquered and slain his successor, Harold Godwinson; and the pure 'English' kings of England were, no doubt to our lasting advantage, for ever of the past.

Two hundred years later comes EDWARD THE FIRST, the first of the numbered Edwards, the greatest of them all. So far.

Heredity hardly foreshadowed his greatness, for he was son of the weakly picturesque Henry the Third and the grasping Eleanor of Provence, not the finest of four famous sisters, queens all four. He was christened in the Confessor's Abbey, which his father was then magnificently rebuilding—turning it into the Abbey we know—and called after the Confessor, the first post-Norman king to bear a pre-Norman name. This marked that the difference between Norman and Saxon, conquerors and conquered, had disappeared; that England now was English.

Still heir to and not wearer of the crown, Edward of Windsor fought on his luckless father's side in the Barons' War. He played the best part in that miserable war. He beat the young Simon de Montfort at Kenilworth and beat and slew the more famous older Simon de Montfort, son of the still more famous and cruel oldest Simon de Montfort, at the cruel battle of Evesham.

188

Still prince, he took the Cross and travelled east against the misbelievers. When amid the ruins of Carthage his uncle Saint Louis died tragically, he became the chief person of the Eighth Crusade. He won the battle of Nazareth. The information that the Emir of Jaffa was longing to turn Christian touched Edward's genuinely pious young heart; he gladly consented to receive the envoy whom the Emir sent to treat of the holy matter, and let him be shewn right into the royal bedroom. It was Edward's birthday. It was summer, a broiling hot evening even for Acre; Edward was sitting on his bed scantily clad. In came the Emir's envoy and, pretending to hand over a letter, aimed instead a poisoned dagger straight at the prince's heart. Edward warded off the blow, got a wound in the arm, snatched the dagger from his enemy and slew him with it. He himself nearly died of his wound; his young wife Eleanor sucked away the poison, and saved his life.

Still abroad, in Sicily, he learned that old Henry III was dead. They proclaimed him king at Paul's Cross on the day of his father's funeral. There was no breach of the King's Peace, and Edward returned to England its acknowledged king.

He became one of its greatest.

He, first, tried to join the three parts of Great Britain into one kingdom. He half succeeded. Wales he won. The redoubtable Llewelyn ap Griffith swore fealty at Rhuddlan and by the *Diktat* of Aberconway was reduced to the rank of a petty chieftain. To appease the Ancient Britons, conquered at last, Edward promised them a prince who should be a native of their country and could speak no word of English; to keep his promise he hurried his queen, near her time, to Caernarvon Castle where she dutifully helped him keep it by giving birth to a son, first Prince of Wales by the Sassenach reckoning. When Llewelyn rebelled again, Edward had his head cut off and set up, wearing a mock crown of willow, on Bridge Gate; that Merlin's prophecy might be fulfilled, and a Welsh prince wear his crown in London.

David's rebellion, and Madog's, and Morgan's, all were crushed, and Edward became the one and effective lord of the Britons.

With Scotland he had less luck. His first plan was to unite the two crowns by betrothing the infant Edward of Caernarvon to the infant Queen of Scots, the Maid of Norway. Despite, or because of, the stock of raisins, figs, walnuts and gingerbread with which Edward provided the good Yarmouth ship sent to Norway to fetch her, the little lady untimely succumbed to the voyage across the North Sea, and so spoilt the plan. Edward's next idea was to choose, among the thirteen warring claimants to the dead Maid's crown who now sprung up, the one most amenable to his unitive dream. There followed the famous and turbulent, savage and heroic, period of

John Balliol and Robert Bruce and William Wallace.

At the New Castle on the Tyne Balliol did homage to Edward as his feudal suzerain; then repented and rebelled. Edward marched north; himself first over the dyke, stormed the then Scottish town—the then greatest Scottish merchant town—of Berwick, and marched on across the Tweed, where Bruce deserted to him and Balliol surrendered.

Victorious Edward removed to England, and placed under the English throne in the Abbey of Westminster, the Sacred Stone of Scone or Destiny. On it the old Gaelic kings had been crowned. On it, ages of the world earlier, the patriarch Jacob's head had rested, that mystical night at Bethel: This is none other but the house of God, and this is the gate of heaven. That same stone of the Dream of Israel— from which the ladder had reached unto the God of Abraham's heaven, His angels ascending and descending on it; which the patriarch's sons had carried into Egypt; which thence (almost everyone lending a hand: Joseph and Pharaoh, and Pharaoh's daughter *Scota*; Cecrops the builder of Athens, and Gathelus of Compostella; Hiberus King of Hibernia, Zedekiah King of Israel; the prophet Jeremiah; St. Aidan, St. Columba . . .) via Spain and the Hill of Tara had unaccountably floated to Scotland—is still in the Abbey, under our throne where Edward I placed it, and above it Edward VIII will be crowned. Let impious geologists assert as they may that the stone belongs to no formation known in Palestine, and is ordinary Scotch sandstone.

Meantime, though war continued, and his arms did fairly well, Edward could not subdue the little northern kingdom. Wallace was in the field.

In English affairs the king allied himself with his people against the barons; and the people, as they should, looked to the Crown as their friend and protector. He made good new laws, and enforced and codified good old ones; his reign counts legally as the most important in our history, the reign which *defined* the Common Law and did more to settle justice than all previous reigns joined together. He was our English Justinian. He put down brigandage and usury, and assured the poor man a larger measure of peace and protection than often has been his lot. With the Model Parliament that he convoked and the Confirmation of the Charters, the English Constitution may be said, as well as at any other time, to have 'begun.'

He ruled England strongly. He ruled it in accordance with the general will; what touches all, he said, should be approved by all. He ruled justly. He ruled. He did what kings are for.

He expelled Israel. Here the people led, and the king for once followed. To appease their anger, he had first tried persecution: made statutes ordering the Jews to wear special badges, preventing them holding real property, forbidding them to employ

Christian servants. It sounds very familiar. Popular clamour, and the monks and the merchants, insisted on more; so Edward drove every Hebrew across the sea.

The better reasons for this drastic deed were the same reasons, if not justifications, as have always led to the oppression of the Jews: their extortionate usury; their bloodsucking of the poor; their help to the big nobles to buy out the little ones; their revelling in their riches, and ostentatious display of their often ill-gotten gains; their scorn, barely hidden beneath the mask of supple servility, of Christian folk and Christian religion. They clipped the coinage, ruined the traders, distrained on the small men, jeered at the Host as it passed their Jewries. The vile hoard of one Aaron of Lincoln was so vast that a special department of the Exchequer had to be created to wind up his affairs: the *Scaccarium Aaronis*. The worse reasons were the same old reasons too: envy, sheer black envy, of the Jews' wealth and ability; black religious hatred and black race hatred; debtors' desire to avoid paying their just debts; Christians' desire to get the Jewish jobs; king's need of their cash. And lying fantastic stories, invented by hate and fear, and embellished by envy; how the Jews kidnapped Christian children, circumcized, crucified, ate them. It all sounds very familiar. Jewish nature has not changed much, nor Christian; nor human nature, nor inhuman.

There was a good deal of sporadic cruelty, both

before and during the expulsion. Beatings-up.
Pogroms. Across seven centuries Primate Peckham
and *Gauleiter* Streicher join Aryan hands, stained with
Israel's blood.

King Edward himself had the Crusader's anti-
Semitism and, like Hitler, seems to have found Jews
distasteful personally. But he was not a cruel man.
Like Hitler, he tried to save them from the worst
excesses of his own policy. He let them take some
of their property out of England with them; he
punished individual deeds of cruelty. A shipmaster
of Queenborough deposited a batch of the exiles on
a sandbank, surrounded by rising waves. When the
wretches prayed him to rescue them he answered:
Call on Moses, who saved you from the Red Sea!
Edward had him punished; it is not stated how.

The last Hebrew was shipped away. Parliament
thanked the King effusively and voted him a fifteenth
in gratitude. For better or worse we had none in
England again till Old Testament Oliver beckoned
them back.

Edward disliked Londoners too. The men of the
capital were jealous of their city's liberties, hostile
to the growth of the royal power, and resentful of
the heavy taxes: the king was always hard up, alike
his Welsh and Scotch wars and his wise English
policies costing money. Also they had insulted his
mother, Eleanor of Provence; cried out at her that
she was a traitress, an adulteress and a *foreigner;* and

194

pelted her with filth, stones and rotten eggs. Edward deprived them of their cherished right of electing their own mayor, and to humble the proud city founded new cities, King's-Town-upon-Hull and New Winchelsea, to be her rivals.

In person the king was royal. Powerful, masculine and handsome; exceedingly tall—"Longshanks"—every inch a king. He had long sinewy arms, and long, strong legs. He had a high forehead; his hair, jet-black in younger days, was at the end snow-white but still luxuriant. He was a skilled swordsman and horseman, a fine example of the mediæval knight, rejoicing in tilt and tournament. He was true to his people and his word—"*Pactum serva*" (Keep troth)—loved his friends and hated his enemies; he was pure, proud and hot-tempered, scornful and snobbish, generous and self-righteous: every inch an Englishman. To his admirable consort, Eleanor of Castile, he was chivalrously devoted and chastely faithful. He was fifteen when he married her, and they were happily married for thirty-five years. When she died, at each spot where her body rested on the way from Lincolnshire to London he set up a beautiful cross to her memory, engraven with her image. Two of the crosses, at Northampton and at Waltham, remain to this day. The most famous of them, near London, his memorial cross to *ma chère reine*—*Charing* Cross—stood till the seventeenth century, when it was destroyed by the Puritan mob.

In a last attempt on Scotland, during a final expedition to put down Robert Bruce, Edward himself died. At Burgh-on-Sands near Carlisle, in sight, but not possession, of Caledonia; while having breakfast in bed. Scotland was not conquered, but he had staked out claims for the future. On his tomb in the Abbey was inscribed:

EDWARDUS PRIMUS SCOTORUM MALLEUS
HIC EST 1308. PACTUM SERVA.

His successor was the child of Caernarvon Castle, unhappy EDWARD THE SECOND.

He was gentle and generous. He was intelligent and gifted. He was the most beautiful man in Christendom. No serf or beggar in any of its monarchies ended life more miserably.

The astrologers had queered his pitch from the start. Expounding the comet which had, in proper cometary tradition, heralded his father's royal birth, they had told his grandmother Eleanor of Provence that, while the bright flames of it foretold a brilliant future for her son, the long train of murky smoke behind it spelt a reign of darkness and disaster for *his* son to come.

Nothing daunted, Second Edward began his reign with the most impressive hallowing any English king had yet known. By comparison of all the pictures, the crown he wore seems the most graceful of the whole regalian series, as befitted his graceful head.

Disastrously for his realm and himself, he did not choose to work at his king's trade. The feudal magnates such as the Earl of Lancaster were no doubt much worse than he was; but it was his job to keep feudal magnates in order, and he did not do it. Government became weak, the barons strong and the people wretched. He taxed heavily, yet failed to administer justice. No statesman, he was no soldier either, and though displaying personal courage there (he had led an earlier charge against the Scots at the age of seventeen), was badly defeated at Bannockburn.

He had delight in music and art, and skill at the manual crafts, and the forge and the anvil. He liked to thatch cottages, dig ditches, to row, walk, saunter; to play games of skill and chance rather than martial games; to sing songs, act plays, make poems. He dabbled in alchemy and mystery. He liked boatmen better than barons. All other courts had male clowns; he perversely, uniquely, his female fool, his *joculatrix*. These were not kingly qualities, least of all in those turbulent days.

He loved only pleasure, and Piers Gaveston—

Come Gaveston,
And share the Kingdom with thy deerest friend.

His glittering royal progresses were the most luxurious sights in English history so far, a delight to his and his Gascon Gaveston's æsthetic souls. The peasants less, who had to pay for the food and the feasting under the polite cover of 'Purveyance,' and fled as the army of pleasure advanced upon them. The Welsh, however, always had a weakness for their Edward of Caernarvon, as he for them.

His queen, Isabella the She-Wolf of France, the very young and cruel and beautiful daughter of cruel Philip le Bel, repaid her lord's slights with interest, in the end by torturing and murdering him. Slights to repay she undoubtedly had. Edward gave the jewels and rings the French king had sent as part of her dowry not to his girl-wife but to his boy-friend, "his good brother Peter," his darling *Pierrot;* to whom, one later day, he gave also the very trinkets she had given him herself. The barons had their grievances too: the wealth and glorious garments and glorious titles— Earl of Cornwall, Duke of Ireland—heaped on the upstart favourite; the rude names the favourite heaped on them: Old Hog, Joseph the Jew, Cuckoo, Black Dog of the Wood.

Queen and barons tried to come to terms with the infatuated man. If he would dismiss Gaveston, stop talking music and magic with him, stop playing chuck-farthing and cross-and-pile (pitch-and-toss) with him, stop giving him kisses and kingdoms, they would cease their opposition. Edward replied:

> *Ere my sweet Gaveston shall part from me*
> *This Ile shall fleete upon the Ocean,*
> *And wander to the unfrequented Inde.*

This was uncompromising. So were the others. And they were tougher. They treacherously captured the beloved, and beheaded him on Blacklow Hill near Warwick.

Then, both sides dissembling, things seemed to go better for a while between husband and wife, though in the land there was lawlessness and famine, and the poor were yet poorer than usual.

But Edward must take to himself another friend, young Hugh le Despenser, who was Lord of Glamorgan. Isabella retorts by taking to herself a paramour, the ferocious Mortimer. Edward offers a thousand pounds for the head of Mortimer; Isabella replies by offering two thousand for the head of Despenser. A minion's worth double a swain. In her tigress rage against a husband insensible, incapable of being sensible, to her charms, Isabella and her lover and their baronial allies at last made open war upon the king. She murdered Despenser; who, in intention at least, was perhaps a reformer, and out to curb feudal disorder. She captured her husband the king, spat at him, made him resign the throne, put him to ride in mock procession on the sorriest nag that could be found, and crowned him with nettles, a king of ignominy and farce.

> *What are kings when regiment is gone,*
> *But perfect shadows in a sun-shine day?*

She placed him prisoner in Berkeley Castle and when blows, starvation, rotting food flung in his face, taunts and torture could not finish him off fast enough, on a dark September night she had him murdered, by a most hideous symbolism of revenge, by a red-hot rod of iron thrust up the wretch's orifice.

The countryfolk heard piteous shrieks in the castle dungeons, shrieks that echoed anew through many dark Septembers afterwards. That horrible distortion of his dead face shewed how he had suffered in dying.

The great poet of later days who shared the king's kink knew best how to describe his degradation. Tragically he makes him say, haggard and starved in the dungeon, at the end:

> *Tell Isabelle the Queene I looked not thus,*
> *When for her sake I ran at tilt in Fraunce*
> *And there unhorst the Duke of Cleremont.*

The son of this miscarried man and his murderess takes, as EDWARD THE THIRD, a considerable place in history.

He succeeded as a boy of fourteen. At seventeen, manhood in those days, he grew tired of the tutelage of his mother and her Mortimer; when the Parliament met at Nottingham, he joined in a plot to rid himself of them. The pair had their suspicions: the Queen went to bed with the keys of the Castle under her pillow, and Mortimer's head upon it. The conspirators got through a secret underground passage, through the solid rock of the Castle hill, into the yard. Amid the Queen's shrieks and tears—"Oh, spare my gentle Mortimer!"—they dragged the paramour out and young Edward had him executed at Tyburn.

This third Edward, yet one more tall and handsome Plantagenet, had a brilliant court, brilliantly described for us by Froissart. He encouraged trade and invited the Flemings to Norwich, to teach us the art of weaving fine cloth. He was ambitious and warlike. He sought to become King of France as well as of England, launching the Hundred Years' War which brought such misery—the 'free companies,' and rapine, and the *Jacquerie*—upon the one country, with no corresponding gain to the other. He was very vigorous and brave. He personally won the fight off Sluys, the first of our long line of sea victories. He personally won the great battle of Cressy—"Let the boy win his spurs," he famously said, when at one moment of the battle his son the Black Prince was in difficulties—where England beat France, and the churl the feudal knight. Moved by the tears of his pregnant queen, Philippa of Hainault, he spared the six burghers of Calais: "Gentle Lady, though I do it against my will, you pray so tenderly that I give them to you." Whether the king had really intended to kill them in revenge for their obstinate courage or whether merely to torture them with the threat of a death he never meant to inflict, history does not certainly reveal; in either case he comes out of the affair badly, as the queen and the burghers well. Tremendously brave, Edward III was always a bit of a brute.

By his French wars he at least stimulated national pride, which may then have needed stimulation.

> *We are conquerors everywhere; nothing*
> *Can stand our soldiers; each man is worthy*
> *Of a triumph. Such an army of heroes*
> *Ne'er shouted to the heavens, nor shook the field.*

He made his obscure island for the first time a victorious and respected name abroad. "When I was young," said Petrarch, "the English were considered the most timid of the barbarians; now they have defeated the warlike French." Edward III in the first part of his reign was a national hero.

He was a rough man, animal and strong; a bold fighting knight. Prodigal and popular; fond of war, feasting, hawking, hunting, and splendour and his own way. He instituted the Order of the Garter, whether fulfilling a vow to restore the Round Table of King Arthur—or because of a lady's leg. *Honi soit qui mal y pense.*

The second half of the reign is darker. Around his extravagant court stalked the horrors of the Black Death, which filled the plague-pits with half England,

and the misery of the peasantry in the last days of decaying feudalism. Taxation was heavy, corruption rampant, John of Gaunt an oppressor; all of France but Calais was lost, and the disbanded soldiery were let loose at home. Edward himself declined into a despised old dotard.

He loved only pleasure, and Alice Perrers: she who received dishonourable mention in our school-books as the harlot and harpy who jinglingly "stripped the rings from the dying king's fingers."

Deserted by her, and by all save one single priest, the hero of Cressy had bare strength to kiss the cross, and to murmur: Jesus, have mercy!

His eldest son the Black Prince died just too soon to become EDWARD THE FOURTH, which title was taken by a much later prince: Edward of York, of March, of Rouen.

He is our first modern-seeming monarch. A Renaissance man rich and magnificent; affable and handsome, indolent and vicious. Not fond of the stuffy older nobility; preferring the merchant princes of London, and their wives. He looked what he was: half hero, half voluptuary; a bloated Bayard.

Too much ill has been said of the fourth Edward, among other English reasons because of the large number of ladies he loved. Remember how he married, as few kings do, for passionate love only: against all his interest, and the wish of the potent

Kingmaker and Last of the Barons. Dame Elizabeth Wydeville (Woodville, our school-books had it) was a poor match, but Edward loved her, and after an unroyally brief acquaintance wedded her and crowned her Queen of England. Perhaps the lady rather forced him into it. Chastely and shrewdly she told the king: "I know I am not good enough to be your queen. But I am too good to become your mistress."

The hint taken, Edward set about improving her status by arranging distinguished marriages for her relations. Her brother John Woodville he was able to wed, as her fourth husband, to the Duchess of Norfolk herself: a skittish damsel of some eighty summers, as William of Worcester skittishly remarks.

How far it was his wife who fixed his 'middle-class' predilections, he certainly preferred the humbler 'made lords' to the great barons of either Roseate complexion. Throughout his most modern reign his motto was: Hard measure for the great, easy measure for the small. London loved him, and he London, much as it loved Charles II two centuries later.

Edward IV was a valiant fighter, in battle from boyhood. He needed to be, for he kept losing his throne and having to win it back: against Margaret of Anjou and the Lancastrians, against Warwick the Kingmaker. It was a bloody business, the factious termination of the Middle Ages in England. When finally, the Last of the Barons slain at Barnet and his corpse carried to London and shewn naked on St.

204

Paul's pavement to the breast so that none might doubt his death, King Edward could breathe, and could say:

> *Once more we sit on England's royal throne,*
> *Re-purchased with the blood of enemies,*

and, weary of war, could ask himself:

> *And now what rests but that we spend the time*
> *With stately triumphs, mirthful comic shows,*
> *Such as befits the pleasure of the court?*

So indeed he spent it: in pomp and plays, with wine and women, eating and drinking. Too fond of pleasure to become the very great king he might have been, he did a good deal to stimulate prosperity and strengthen government. Too lazy and too jovial to be a very bad king, it was he who introduced instruments of tyranny that were to be the worst side of the subsequent Tudor kingship: terrorism, interference with the course of justice, spies, the rack. He had his brother the Duke of Clarence poisoned with a cup of Malmsey wine, or (the version we all prefer) drowned in a butt of it. He gained popularity by his lavish expenditure, and lost it by the taxes he imposed to meet that expenditure. He was up to date and befriended Caxton, giving him £20. Despite the wretched Roses he kept fair order among the barons.

For whatever reason—his many mistresses, his mighty
meals—he had the heaviest doctor's bill of any king
in English history.

In ballad and popular story, Edward of York's chief
fame is his love for the ladies; Charles II being his
one rival, as Nell Gwynne is Jane Shore's. The King
said: "I have three Mistresses, one the Merriest,
another the Cunningest, and a third the Holiest in
the Kingdom." The last was indeed so holy that she
could never be dragged out of church save to go to
bed, and vice versa, and divided her time exclusively
between copulation and confession. The first was
Jane Shore, merry Jane the goldsmith's wife.

Why should we boast of Laius and his Knights,
Knowing such Champions entrapt by Whorish Lights?
Or why should we speak of Thais's curled Locks,
Or Rhodope that gave so many Men the P—x?
Read in old Stories, and there you will find,
How Jane Shore, Jane Shore, *she pleased King* Edward's
Mind.

     Jane Shore she was for England, Queen Fredrick
        was for France,
     Sing Honi soit qui mal y pense.

Of the old Amazons it were too long to tell,
And likewise of the Thracian Girls, how far they did excel;
Those with the Scythian lads engaged in several Fights,
And in the brave Venerean Wars did foil adventurous Knights;

Messalina and Julia were Vessels wond'rous brittle;
But Jane Shore, Jane Shore, *took down King* Edward's
    mettle.
        Jane Shore she was for England, etc.

Hellen of Greece she came of Spartan Blood,
Agricola and Cresside they were brave Whores and good;
Queen Clytemnestra boldly slew old Arthur's mighty Son;
And fair Hesione pull'd down the Strength of Telamon.
Those were the Ladies that caus'd the Trojan Sack,
But Jane Shore, Jane Shore, *she spoiled King* Edward's
    Back.
        Jane Shore, etc.

Maresia of Italy, see how she stoutly copes
With Jesuits, Priests, Cardinals, and tripple Crowned Popes;
And with King Henry Rosamund spent many a dallying
    Hour,
'Till lastly poyson'd by the Queen in Woodstock fatal Bower;
And Joan of Ark play'd in the Dark with the Knights of
    Languedock,
But Jane Shore *met King* Edward *and gave him Knock*
    for Knock.
        Jane Shore, etc.

The jolly Tanner's Daughter, Harlot of Normandy,
She only had the Happiness to please Duke Robert's Eye;
And Roxalina, tho' a Slave, and born a Grecian,
Could with a Nod, command and rule Grand Signior Soliman;

And Naples Joan would make them groan, that ardently
  did lov'r,
But Jane Shore, Jane Shore, *King* Edward *he did shove'r.*
    Jane Shore, etc.

Hamlet's incestuous Mother was Gathernard, Denmark's
  Queen,
And Circe, that enchanting Witch, the like was scarcely
  seen;
Warlike Penthesilea was an Amazonian Whore
To Hector and young Troilus, both which did her adore;
But brave King Edward, *who before had gained nine*
  Victories,
Was like a Bond-slave fetter'd within Jane Shore's
  All-conquering Thighs.
    Jane Shore she was for England, Queen Fredrick
      was for France,
    Sing Honi soit qui mal y pense.

Never was a royal strumpet more gentle and
generous than Jerking Jane. She passed her days in
deeds of kindness and mercy; in helping her friends,
and the poor and unhappy. A good woman.

"Let not poor Nelly starve," said Charles Stuart
dying. Edward Plantagenet begged the same for poor
Jane. But as soon as he was safely dead, her enemies
got her, and the base envious friends she had been
good to got her—the priests and the puritans and
Richard Crookback got her—and after suffering

indignities and cruelties at their hands, far too many to tell of here, it is of starvation in the end that she died, in a ditch: Shore-ditch.

EDWARD THE FIFTH was son of the foregoing Edward and Elizabeth Woodville.

He was the elder of the two little Princes in the Tower, smothered in their sleep by the foul orders of Uncle Crookback. He 'reigned' five months; in the Tower.

Although Henry VIII was so manly and had those world-famous six wives, between the seven of them they could only produce one single male child, the short-lived unmanly EDWARD THE SIXTH.

This boy was unpleasingly precocious, knowing all his Latin declensions and conjugations at seven, translating Cicero from Latin into Greek at thirteen; a fanatic proselyte of the new religion, in whose name its name was tarnished; a puppet, perhaps a rather unhappy one, in the hands of the robber lords Somerset and Northumberland, who bribed him with books and flattery, and the pleasures of persecution of the Catholics, and pocket-money. He seems to have been a young prig. He engaged in lengthy ostentatious prayer. He adored sermons. He admired Cranmer. A playfellow brought him a Bible to stand upon, to enable him to fetch down some object out of reach, and he reproved him in an edifying speech.

When his whipping-boy Barnaby Fitzpatrick visited France, Edward adjured him *never*, in that frivolous land, to neglect daily reading of the Holy Scriptures.

These may, of course, be mere slanders; invented, with intention the opposite of slanderous, by later Puritans to turn the poor lad, the first prince of their persuasion, into a paragon worthy of the part.

A good thing for everyone that he died young. Or, on the contrary, a bad thing? The despotism and ultra-Protestantism he was heading for might, if he had lived, have caused a reaction against both and prepared the way for a freer England and a moderate and united Catholic England; which his bitter bigoted sister coming too soon—coming at all—made impossible. Seen through the balefires of her reign, his violent one contrived to wear the halo of a golden age.

For the extreme Protestants he was the Supreme Head of the Church, the successor of Peter; for the extreme Romanists the supreme enemy of the Church, the successor of Nero. The intolerance of the modern age had begun.

He died in the odour of sanctity, a little Lamb of God, according to the one party; in quite another kind of odour, according to the other party, in the degradation of a scaly skin disease and pungent rotting of his whole scarecrow body, that was God's vengeance upon him and his heretic syphilitic sire.

One side still had exclusive possession of the text-

books when we were young. In my youthful enthusiasm youthful Edward was a pure hero: the good
wistful boy-king who hated Papists, and served nobly
the pure faith, a saint seen saintlier in the tigress
shadow that came after. I went too far in my enthusiasm. Edward VI was not a good boy-king: one
grade lower—a good-boy king.

Distinctly different, on any evaluation, was
EDWARD THE SEVENTH, son of Queen Victoria and
Prince Albert of Saxe-Coburg, who reigned from
1901 to 1910. It is a jump of three and a half centuries
and of fourteen reigns from his last namesake, from
boy of the other world to man very much of this,
and meantime the world has become the modern
world and the kingdom has spread from one part of
one little island to the imperial seven seas.

A jump of only a quarter-century, and only one
reign, and next——

EDWARD
VIII

I

ASOOTHSAYER foretold that young Victoria would have the longest and, till then, most glorious reign in English history; that two shorter reigns would follow, of kings; that a third king then would arise, whose reign would be even as glorious as her own. His name would be David.

When strange old Lady Waterford lay waiting to die (and saw visions, and England and Israel united once again) she sent imploring that the heir in the fourth generation, then waiting to be born, should if a son bear the son of Jesse's name. The Royal Family humoured her: gave the child the names of all four of the British patron saints. David they put at the end. It moved prophetically forward, to become the name the family addressed him by, and by which he secretly addressed himself.

He was born at White Lodge in Richmond Park on June 23rd, 1894; between the Victorian Jubilees; between forty-two and forty-three years ago.

The first great-grandson of a reigning queen ever to be born. An interesting point, and there were others, but on the whole his arrival was not much dwelt upon. The Queen would live for years, decades, centuries yet. The hour of this infant of the fourth generation seemed mythically far away.

Parliament, however, duly sent an address of congratulation to Her Majesty; only Keir Hardie protesting. "I do not," he said, "owe allegiance to any hereditary ruler, and I consider that this resolution elevates to an importance it does not deserve an event of everyday occurrence. In the interest of the dignity of this House I take leave to protest. From his childhood upwards this puling royal great-grandchild" (five days old) "will be surrounded by sycophants and will be taught to believe himself a superior creature."

The last part of the rather lovable agitator's speech was scarcely fulfilled. The puling royal great-grandchild was brought up to believe himself, in all ways but the magical one, an ordinary and not superior creature. With George and Mary on the watch, sycophants did not encircle.

In 1901, on the death of his great-grandmother, he became heir-presumptive.

In 1910, after an upper-class childhood as normal as George and Mary could make it, on the death of his grandfather whom he adored he became the heir.

In 1911, at the age of seventeen, he was made Prince of Wales; twentieth to bear that famous title.

The youth became a personage, and generous copy for the newspapers. He began his life in the terrible limelight and to create, and have created for him, that personality as The Prince which for the next quarter-century was to be so prominent in Press and public imagination, and perhaps his own imagination also.

It is not known how far the Press prince and the prince of the public imagination—similar, not quite the same—were the same as the prince of his own.

Until I was twenty and he eighteen I had hardly ever thought about him. I was no royalist, I was an ardent radical; I had arrived in Oxford from a very different world.

We learnt that he was coming up. The news was not exciting; but it was reasonably interesting. Unimportant though royalty might be, it was right and proper that the young man should be sent to Oxford instead of the other place.

Victoria, the elder Edward, George the new king, his queen Mary, were stereotyped visions on calendars, stamps, coins, in books and newspapers. I found that I thought upon two only of the royal faces as faces of real human beings: Queen Alexandra's with its goodness and beauty, so superior to the funny Brunswick women; and this gentle boy's, so different from his undistinguished and indistinguishable little brothers.

I recalled the first time I had seen—remembered I had seen—a picture of him. A mild-eyed child, wistful wisp of a small person, in a sailor suit;

younger than I was by a year or two, and very much better-looking. As I had looked at the picture—rather surprised, with my infantile hatred of kings, that a king's son should look so tender and kind instead of majestic and haughty—I had felt, who was never of an envious turn, no envy of the other child's fairer face, but only a liking and secret understanding.

Years afterwards old Edward died, and young Edward had been for the first time the centre of a ceremony; the papers had had long articles about him, and photographs. Before the fairy-tale battlements of Caernarvon Castle his father the King had presented him, a Galahad boy gloriously apparelled, to the assembled Welsh people as their prince. The ceremony was wonderful, I had thought, with my raw romantic sympathy for the dispossessed Ancient Britons; and so was he. I date my royalism from then.

Thus meditating when I heard that next Michaelmas —1912—he would be coming up, I mildly hoped I should have a glimpse of him.

The hope was at once fulfilled. Term had hardly begun when I learnt that he would be attending our opening debate at the Union Society. The motion was a straight party one: No Confidence in His Majesty's Government—Asquith's. I, as a leading Liberal light of the undergraduate world, was set to make the principal speech against the motion. Before the debate our President, Gordon Woodhouse (killed in the War), brought the Prince along and presented a few of us to him. We shook hands shyly; on both sides. He was smaller than I had imagined him, and more Germanic-looking; timid and tiny; a straw-blond very slight figure in a navy-blue serge suit.

We formed a little procession across the garden into the Debating Hall, Woodhouse and the Prince leading. As we entered, the house stood up and (I think) cheered.

Where to seat him had been a problem. In the Union, as in its prototype the House of Commons, the two sides sit sharply divided, sheep and goats facing each other on opposite sides of the hall. For His Majesty's heir the faintest appearance of favouring, or not favouring, His Majesty's Government had to be avoided. We could not put him on a stool between the rival benches. He could not occupy the President's throne. We could not set him in mid-air. Gordon Woodhouse solved the problem by putting him on the 'committee bench' on the right-hand side of the house, the for-the-motion (that night the Tory) side, and bidding me, as the night's chief Radical, sit with my opponents on that bench and next the Prince; dividing him and them.

J. G. Lockhart, the opener, made his speech. When I had made mine, and sat down again beside our guest, he congratulated me; a smile, and a shy murmured word or two.

I told him how we ran the debates. He was not,

I thought, very interested; but he fairly successfully strove to appear so, and asked me questions and made one or two comments. He was slightly bored with it all; us all. Even more in awe of us than we of him. He wished he was not there; he hoped very soon he would not be. He was nervous, and nibbled at his nails and looked downwards. At any amusing points in speeches or in my remarks which *sotto voce* accompanied them he brightened up, however, and smiled a quite extraordinarily attractive smile.

My feelings were compounded of pride in sitting next to the Prince of Wales; disapproval of such pride and zeal in hiding it; desire to behave appropriately, desire to please him, active pleasure in his smile and company; sympathy, pity, shame; pride in sitting next to the Prince of Wales. It was rather beastly to be making this frightened boy come among us to be bored by us, to be greedily looking at him while furtively and Englishly pretending not to. It was pleasanter *not* to be the Prince of Wales.

He escaped when he decently could. Whether through the Aye door or the No door I don't remember, but he saved the Crown of England's impartiality by calling in a clear voice as he passed out: "No vote!"

I met him one other time, at a dinner party given by Gilbert Talbot, Toc H. (killed in the war), where he sat virginally awkward; battling again, mouth set, to hide and conquer his dis-ease in the company of us talking fellows. And I saw him one other time: in heavy rain in a mackintosh walking quickly alone under the Broad Street wall of Exeter, a solitary elusive figure.

That Union evening I was grafting the pictures of earlier memory on to the Prince who was beside me, and vice versa. I was creating my vision of him. It is still my vision of him: a vision of youth and innocence; modesty with dignity; of a very young man nervous, nervy, and yet brave; loving, but not loved enough; most unusually good-natured and attractive; with a sense of fun, but prevailing sadness. Prince or no prince—and I still half-heartedly, because of his rank, tried to be prejudiced *against* him—he was, on his own as a human being, one of the most likeable persons on whom I had looked.

The two outward signs were the smile, composed of humour, understanding and kindness; and the eyes, gentle, evasive a little, and unhappy. The word for the tragic quality of their sadness I did not find until many years later—until after I had begun this book—in the writings of one of the intimates of royalty. That acute observer remarked that to no ancestor of the House of Hanover—to which indeed! —could he trace the *Weltschmerz* in the little Prince's eyes.

He was an object of mild interest to us at Oxford. We exchanged jokes and stories about him: good-natured stories, never discreditable to him and not

often to us. There were tales of his musical and
sporting feats: how he made such a noise on the
bagpipes that his college authorities had had to ask,
humbly order, him to abandon the use of that
instrument; how he gave an acceptable vocal render-
ing of the Red Flag, accompanying himself on the
banjo; how, if at the swaggerer Oxford sports known
to most of us only by hearsay, such as hunting and
polo, he was in a high class, at those we knew better
he was less proficient, scraping into but the Magdalen
Second Eleven at Soccer and rising to bare corporality
in the O.T.C. On him, so girlishly guiltless in
appearance, and his tall masculine tutor Mr. Hansell
who gallantly chaperoned him up and down the
High, we bestowed the joint joyful nickname of
Hansel and Gretel. The infinite gyratory abasements
were described thanks to which, it was averred—
no doubt quite slanderously—the great President
of Magdalen had secured him for that college to the
discomfiture of Christ Church, royalty's traditional
haunt. Christ Church men affected indifference to,
or even guarded approval of, His Majesty's choice.
"After all," said one of them, "in these democratic
days it is only right and proper that the heir to the
throne should get to know *all* classes of his future
subjects." The infinite racial adroitness was commented on whereby a certain fellow-undergraduate
so frequently succeeded in appearing beside him in
photographs of college groups. There was the

222

Jacobite stalwart—I knew the ass—who rammed his hat down on his head, when the Prince with the Queen, up for the day to visit her son, usurpingly passed by. Another (Guelphite) undergraduate knocked the hat off. There was the female citizen of a great free country that has no truck with kings who tried to clamber up the wall and peep into his rooms. There was that male fellow-citizen of hers who accosted a young man in Magdalen front quad and begged him to point out the Prince: "There he is!" said the Prince obligingly, pointing to a grave Indian in a turban who happened to pass by. To yet another of that republican race (on whom, by the Motherland's generosity, all such stories are automatically fathered) the great Georgian building of Magdalen was pointed out as the Prince's private residence while in Oxford, and the deer in the Deer Park as beasts specially imported from the Pyrenees, expense no object, for him to hunt.

A few fools there were, harmless climbers on the social ladder, who would announce that they knew the Pragger-Wagger *well*, and had always *just* been having brekker or lunch with him. Whether privately envied or not, they were either squashed or else listened to with that indifference that masks, while it meetly punishes, snobbery.

Really there was very little snobbery. We hardly thought about him, the king's son among us; we had more interesting things to think about. The watchword was, Leave him in peace. At Oxford, he did have peace. And freedom: from ceremony, crowds, staring. Maybe more freedom than he has had anywhere since.

I suppose there was a detective; we never detected him.

II

War broke out; and there is the story, probably true story, of the young man's desire to go to the Front and of Kitchener's point-blank refusal. It was not that he wanted to die; or indeed to live. A prickly conscience would not let him be, would not suffer him in peace of mind to escape the risks and rigours that every other young man who wanted to was facing.

"What if I am killed? I have four brothers."

"Oh, if *that* were the only danger," answered K. of K., with the grim smirk that did for a smile, "you could probably go. But I decline to face the risk of your being taken prisoner."

As the War dragged on and hundreds of thousands of young men were killed, and maimed, there was criticism of the authorities for not sending him, the most exalted of the young men, out into the battle. Criticism would have been louder if they *had* sent him.

Compelled to elude danger, he sought drudgery. He mastered army details, and became a good regimental officer. In France he took as active a part as his masters permitted; if, in his own word, that part was certainly "insignificant."

Peace broke out; and in 1919, around him the thrones falling, in that hour of unrest when heirs to them seemed out of place, and date, at twenty-five and absurdly young for it he began in earnest his public and publicized Prince of Wales-hood.

On his imperial tours he was seen of more subjects than any previous heir to the throne. He travelled more widely through his empire than any previous prince in history. More widely than Hadrian; more economically, without that vast retinue; more respectably, without Antinous.

If you are destined, or doomed, to become the head and figure-head of a giant Empire, how better employ yourself until your hour than by seeing and knowing as much as you can of its places and peoples, and giving to as many of them as possible the chance of knowing or seeing you? Royalty in training, he was royalty functioning; sharing the work, temporally and spatially too much for any one man, of his father the King.

He succeeded with both the important people and the People. In Canada alike with Government House and his 'fellow-Albertans,' neighbours at his

225

ranch. A railway strike threatened to hold him up in New Zealand. The strikers sent a message that for him they would make an exception: his train alone would run. A petty incident—or unique in history? Do republican strikers do so for their beloved Presidents? In India, one day as the boy's car was driving along a hot dusty road, he saw, huddled apart, in forlorn degradation by the roadside, a group of Untouchables, the most wronged and wretched of sub-mankind. No one had told him they were there. But he saw the misery in their eyes (there is misery in his own), and turning towards them, the King-Emperor's son stood up in his car as he passed them, at the salute.

For all the adulation, in our hearts we underpraise princes. To their station is attributed achievement that sometimes is owing to themselves. The Prince of Wales, I think, never received his due as the individual young man, who with no power or legions but only himself, came, saw and conquered an Empire; breathed life, and love, into the wise paper provisions of the Statute of Westminster; did more than any other person, Parliament or parchment to make the union of the British peoples under the British Crown seem a living reality.

It was partly the bare fact of his presence; partly the fortunate accident of his personality. He might so easily have failed, or but half succeeded. When that very young man set out, alone, on his first empire journey, many in London were anxious as to the outcome. The most anxious will have been himself.

At the end of heavy days he could speak only in a whisper, and his hand was helpless and swollen from their pitiless democratic hand-shaking. The nervous strain was worse than the physical:—the endless new scenes, new faces, the endless crowds, endless cheering, staring, mobbing; the new hundreds every week to talk to, freshly, as for them alone, as though their supreme moment was his also; the new millions to smile at, be neared by, peered at, cheered by. He, who by original nature disliked it all, must be the Symbol for longer on end, more intensively and extensively, in the eyes and hearts of more people, more peoples, than any human being in history.

The authorities—King George, or Lloyd George, or whoever it was—should have rested him more. The psychological fatigue of those touring years he took years to recover from; has never quite recovered from.

Mr. H. G. Wells pronounced the Prince's "smiling tours" to be "a propaganda of inanity unparalleled in the world's history." Mr. Wells knows about the world's history; he has written books about it; no doubt had the whole of it clearly and steadily in mind when he gave utterance to words so portentous. The stale old writing man complained that the fresh young royal man had not made of his progresses a "re-statement of the obligations and duties of Empire."

Whatever that may have meant, Wales (whose pilloried smile, by the way, was one thousand million times pleasanter than Wells's) had to confine himself to what was possible. It was considerable. The British imperial tie is, so most British hold, as political facts go a more desired and desirable political fact than most. The Prince's duty was, by appearing, to strengthen it. Which he did—with a comparative absence of inanity not often paralleled in the world's history.

To foreign countries—France, the States, the Argentine—Prince Charming approved himself a more valuable ambassador than any that the republics themselves had.

At home, the selection of duties they made for him, and that in part he was able to make for himself, was quite a good selection.

As President of the British Legion, he inspired much of what was done for the ex-soldier. At that hospital for permanently disabled men which he was visiting, the authorities tried to keep him away from the worst rooms: Worst Room. There, apart, dwelt a human being still just human; blind, dumb; without legs or arms; almost without face; a form that could utter guttural sounds indicating hunger or pain; a shapeless trunk that still was 'alive.' He—it —had been found between the lines; whether Englishman, Frenchman, German nobody knew.

They tried to keep the Prince out. He forced his way in, to be alone with the other. When the officials came and he had to take his leave, he bent over the other and on the forehead *kissed* him.

As Patron of the National Council of Social Service he helped another main category of the war's victims, the unemployed. He broke finally with the tradition that monarchy is more the affair and the friend of the fortunate. Up and down England, in the blackest wintriest places of England, he visited hundreds of unemployed men's clubs. The political cure for the evil was not, by our Crown's curious destiny, his business. That was for his father's succeeding governments, Conservative or Labour. Non-political remedy, the human action of "neighbours and friends" the young Prince, better than any man, was in a position to stimulate. It was for the Government to see the ugly problem as a whole. Edward said: "Let us break it up into little pieces." And on local lines the work, the best done in England since the war, under his active working patronage proceeded.

It is possible to over-estimate the use and importance of all such royal participations. It is possible to under-estimate them.

The political people did not always make his task easy. On his tour through desolate Durham, when for the first time he found himself face to face with the miners' misery—with what the world is like—at once he cancelled all the dinners and receptions, sent away his suite, and under the guidance of the Socialist miners themselves went down the mines, into the hovels, about among the poverty and hunger and filth. He told the journalists what he had seen and what he thought. They were not allowed to print it. The Government stopped his tour.

"Some of the things I see in these gloomy poverty-stricken areas make me ashamed to be an Englishman."

When he tried, next, to see South Wales on his own conditions, the Government demurred. He refused to accept their official programme of festivities and selected aspects. The Government insisted. He refused to go.

In the General Strike of 1926 they were not able to prevent his subscribing to the Miners' Distress Fund.

He had functions and ceremonies and official obligations of every sort. He cannot always have found them interesting; with no royal illusions, he indeed over-estimated their futility at first. He performed them all well.

He went up in aeroplanes, down coal mines, over shipyards, into slums, out with fishing fleets.

He acquainted himself with many men and matters. A certain part of his time he devoted to study; but true to the family tradition got little, even too little, out of books. He swotted languages; Spanish successfully. He studied faces, and became the good

judge of them that his own youthful face continued
to belie.

He amused himself.

Jazz, dancing, films, gramophone, bagpipes,
ukulele.

At some sports, such as flying, he was very good;
at others not so good. A fearless, a reckless rider, he
had many falls and once broke his collar-bone. There
were protests in Parliament—complimentary protests
really, shewing that he was thought a national asset
not lightly to be risked. He used the argument he
had tried with Kitchener:—I have plenty of brothers;
the succession is not in danger. The King gave ear to
the protests. The Prince protested in his turn. He
had less personal freedom than any other young man
of fortune, and here was one of the few purely private
pleasures left to him being meddled with. He stood
out for a while; in the end gave in; and gave up
steeple-chasing.

He acquired an immense personal popularity;
an authentic popularity, not living by publicity.
Rather did publicity live by it. It never turned his
head, which was as sound as his heart. This popularity
he never lost, if slight curious ups and downs in it
were detectable. When his father at last came into
his own—in those years from King George's first illness, through the Jubilee, to the end—awhile Edward
seemed to be a little less the first idol of a monarchy-
idolizing people. The two men appealed, on their

personal side, to such different emotions of the English
that it would have been hard for them to hold first place
together. George at the end rightly held first place.

In those fifteen years publicity assumed an intensity
and a ferocity not hitherto known. Unlike quite a
few of the royals, the Prince hated it. He hated the
clicking cameras. Every word he said was seized by
popular press and by wireless; every movement he
made was spied on for the films. Probably this was
the aspect of his fate he jibbed at the most.

I say 'probably.' What in the name of heaven
do I know about it, who am holding forth so glibly?
What do most people *know* about these people?

The fierce light that beats upon a throne does not
illumine; it dazzles and obscures. The reality of
royalty is not seen.

What the true Prince was like I merely do not
know: what his points were, good or bad. The
following list is a guess-list.

Common sense. In dealing with men, uncommon
sense. Humour, over underlying sadness. The usual
kingly qualities of tact, tolerance, physical courage.
Moral courage. The quality, not more usual in
kings than other people, of pure goodness of heart.
Generosity: pity. Inability—moral incapacity—to
be mean or cruel. Intelligence above the average in
some directions: where men and their motives
were concerned; where memory played a part;

232

regarding machinery and all mechanisms. A clear-cut charming individuality. A dominating sense of duty. An absence absolute of insincerity.

Defects? The ineradicable royal one of dislike of opposition and remonstrance. Impatience of excuses and delays; a nervous irritated quality in the impatience. Obstinacy, which sometimes skirted danger: wanting his own way, and put out when he did not get it; getting it, sometimes, when better not to. Nervous youthful need of perpetual distraction. Pleasure in any kind of company that provided it. Ordinary failings of flesh and spirit.

Omissions? Without base flattery, nobody I think could have called him artistically or intellectually gifted, or have attributed to him a subtle, remarkable, or specially interesting mind. The concerns of one ardent minority of his future subjects—in books, art, music (decent music), the passion of ideas—nobody imagined him to share.

At the age of forty he had not heard of the great writer who was Charlotte Brontë. One of his few friends with literary tastes put *Jane Eyre* into his hand. An hour later a member of his entourage, a reading man, came in. "What is this *appalling* stuff?" exclaimed the Prince, "and who *is* this Charlotte *Bront?*" "One of the greatest of English novelists, Sir," replied the other gravely; who, a Haworth enthusiast, could yet see that that strange book compounded of genius, impossible sentiment

233

and roaring melodrama might appear to a novice richly to deserve the adjective which that particular imperial novice applied to it.

He had neither a commanding intellect, a commanding presence, nor a commanding personality. He was as well without them; given the peculiar requirements of the constitutional and representative kingship ahead.

Going on guessing, I should say the Prince of Wales was a youth who would never have chosen that destiny of ordered duty in the glare and glitter, under millions of staring eyes; to whom, alike highly-strung and humble-minded, un-royal peace and freedom would have been peculiarly dear. He hated the fuss and fawning; the monotony of majesty. He hated the clicking cameras. He longed for the right to live his own life which every one of the King's subjects but himself possessed and, in hours of depression, longed for escape from fate and the throne ahead. "It was the Devil."

The nervous young man set his teeth. Having no honourable choice but to bear the burden he was born to bear, he steeled himself to bear it bravely; to feel boredom no more than he has ever shewn it; to enjoy what he could not alter; what he had to do, to do well.

The eyes still tragic.

No equality. More rights than other men, or less. If attacked, as subterraneously he sometimes was, he could not hit back. As, at Dartmouth, other boys might be cheeky with him but not he with them, so later he could not get even with critics or scandal-mongers. No give and take.

No margin of error allowed. Mistakes, when he made them, magnified. All life lived under the monstrous monarchic magnifying glass; the World peering through.

No real freedom in choosing his friends. Caste and convention put barriers on one side, the defects (including his own) of human nature on the other: how could he be sure of the complete disinterested-ness of *anyone* whom he might desire in friendship? He had some amusing fast companions. A perfect friend was what he desired, and needed, the most.

There was development. By the end of prince-hood he had contrived to overcome his inherent distaste for many of the inherencies of his position. In earlier days, for example, making speeches had been an agony; he forced himself into becoming a good and easy speaker, much the best of the family. He schooled himself to enjoy crowds, and to tolerate ceremonial. A boyish tie-fingering shyness remained late. He rid himself almost entirely of that also, and became the self-controlled man of the world it was desirable for him and for the world he should become. He adapted the ancient tradition he stood for to his own modern outlook; on the whole taking, and giving, the best of both.

The estimate here may be false, or foolish; on Living Kings little that is written escapes the one fault or the other. Down one of the princely pitfalls—snobbery, inverted snobbery; ignorance, irrelevance; triviality, banality—or more than one, every such writer is bound headlong to go. I have tumbled, I know, down them all.

It is a superficial estimate; of how he, the human being, secretly in his own mind and soul fitted in, or did not fit in, with his preposterous position, it says (as it knows) nothing.

I think it is an under-estimate. It does not fairly adumbrate the charm, or pathos, or courage of this man.

If, however, it is on balance a favourable estimate, not only pleasure in princes as such has made it so. I, this humble subject and writer, should not have expressed nor have felt—nor, I believe, would a majority have felt—quite the same degree, or quality, of pleasure in any of his royal brothers who might in his place have been Prince of Wales. Delighted to honour king's sons, England would have made the most of the evident qualities of each, and have accorded them deserved respect and popularity. The deep note of affection that was for Edward would have been absent.

In one brother we should have discerned the qualities of integrity and devotion to duty, and happiness found in a model marriage, and plain

236

English goodness, that we saw and esteemed in King George; of whose reign his own would have bid fair to be a worthy and excellent continuance. With another, bluff and soldierly, we should—with a rather different emphasis—have made ourselves content. In the third brother again, with his youth, zest and good looks, our loyalist appetite would have had ample to feed upon. All three would have had the advantage over their eldest brother of gracious consorts, on whom no sleek paragraphers or slick photographers could have conferred good lives and good looks they had been wholly without. All would have been good Princes of Wales.

The one chance gave was better. He was the most successful Prince of Wales in history.

III

On January 20th, 1936 he became THE KING.

No tremor or shadow of doubt as the succession passed.

Holding his first Privy Council, he said: "When my Father stood here twenty-six years ago He declared that one of the objects of His life would be to uphold constitutional government. In this I am determined to follow in My Father's footsteps and to work as He did throughout His life for the happiness and welfare of all classes of My Subjects.

I place My reliance upon the loyalty and affection of My peoples throughout the Empire, and upon the wisdom of their Parliaments, to support Me in this heavy task, and I pray that God will guide Me to perform it."

During the year almost since he spoke those words, he has answered the hopes they aroused. The antique institution has worked well.

A new reign is a landmark, if only because we English think it one. By contrast with the Heads, the grotesquely different Heads, of the other great lands, Edward stands a sign of hope in the darkness and devilment around. He is one of the hopeful human figures of this hour.

Politically, his position has not so far acquired importance. Nowadays a youngish King of England is unlikely to play a decisive role at the beginning of his reign; and, at home, it has not been a year of decisive events. His routine duties—the ceremonies, reviews, progresses, audiences, documents—he has fulfilled quite perfectly; although, without Consort or Prince of Wales, he has had less help near the throne than any predecessor for over a century. He has, indeed, been doubling the parts of King and Prince: in the Welsh derelict areas the other day, which was he?

A fear that he would eschew pomp and ceremony, 'democratically' espousing an undesired extreme simplicity, has been belied. Kings have to be KINGS, and he knows it; while aware of changes which the times demand and willing, almost too willing, to make them.

He will shed the Crown's last remnant of class affiliation: to stand, equally, as the representative of all portions of the people. He will destroy the last lingering notion that the King is for the mighty, and promotes or prefers their policies. Associated, as formal headship must be, with the fighting services, the Crown worn by this highly civilian Edward will shew itself less predominantly bound up with those; to appear, equally, as the crown of the country's peaceful endeavour.

He will win from the working classes a warmer adherence to his office. He is from his heart devoted to their interests. They like him from their hearts better than any king remembered.

Youth, though he is himself so curiously young, I doubt if he will in the same way win: make the Throne the needed rallying-point, inspiration, banner for the idealism of Young England, now watered and weakly dispersed between a dozen variant strivings: Scouts, Oxford Group, Labour League of Youth; Territorials, League of Nations Union, Youth Hostels Association; hiking, slumming; sport, social service, what not else. . . . Democracies—with kings or without them—do not seem able to use, much less enthuse, human beings aged under twenty-five; as the dictatorships can. Mussolini, Lenin, Hitler, whatsoever their compensating crimes, won the devotion of their nations' youth; through which, and not only through bludgeons and philosophies of blood, they won.

Besides, unfortunately, among the young people of England Edward does not know the idealists.

Will he last?[1]

It seems quite likely. He seems to be fulfilling the king-need, which is not less strong than it was, not less well than any predecessor. He is an immense success, and hope. The antique institution is working well.

Individuality, a forward-looking spirit, radical sympathy and sincerity in the Person give expectation that the Institution will be of use in days soon ahead; that monarchy may be the monarchy of the last fifty years, and even a little more; the little more that may be needed. Some conservatives (small c) are anxious about him. Among that half of the people that is, traditionally, less keen on kings, there is more keenness—and interest, and hope, and love—than for centuries.

"The first king who tried to rule unconstitutionally, or made one very bad mistake, or led a vicious life, would," a sour prophet has half-hopefully been warning us, "be also the last." It may be so. Edward VIII is not likely to be that king.

Mistakes, no doubt, he will make. In his peculiar

[1] Written November, 1936.

isolation—he has no one who is both friend and experienced counsellor, neither in his Family nor his Government; there are no Elder Statesmen for him to turn to in an hour of need, as there were Rosebery, Balfour and others when his father acceded; he has no wise old man-of-the-world crony among any of the political people, no friend or familiar at all among the older generation, political or other—it will be peculiarly hard for him not to make a few.

England is with him in his *resolve*, scarcely shared by the present Cabinet, to alleviate the misery of and build a future for the black derelict places. But he must be careful, tiptoe careful, not to try to realize his resolve in any fashion that the watchful reactionaries of the present Cabinet—noble democratic defenders of the people against royal encroachment and human pity—could pounce upon as 'unconstitutional.'

Mistakes, no doubt, he has already made.

In this twelvemonth almost, gossips have had time to gossip; to wag tongues, and heads; to air small grievances and preferences. Preferences for this thing the King has done over the other thing; for the old King—for this reason, for that reason—over the new King; or vice versa. Grievances in respect of that or this omission, or commission, which outrages the particular gossiper's particular prejudices.

In one case a prejudice not particular, but universal.

Plainly, 1936 has been too *royal* a time for that

raffish group that now lords it over London society, that moneyed pack of (mainly) immigrant aliens, naturalized or otherwise, the Invaders, the most heartless and dissolute of the pleasure-loving ultra-rich, the hardest and most hated people in England. Names, published for all to see, of guests honoured by Majesty with gracious invitations—honoured, still more signally, with invitations accepted by Majesty—have included names that even the man in the street knows about, and knows nothing to admire; a high proportion of such names; higher than the names of the King's subjects mere British-born.

These peoples' sympathies, if they had any, are the antithesis of the King's own deepest sympathies.

Yet be chary of judging. By paradox, the un-patriotic-looking frequentation of this company may be patriotism. It may be that only there, in the curious contrast of its at least vibrant atmosphere, he can discover and drink in the vitality that he daily desperately needs to sustain his crushing role.

The job, the fantastic tremendous position, the high headship of five hundred million people, Emperor-King, *Idol* of one fourth of the earth, is almost intolerable. A highly-strung, original man can only bear it if he has, as outlet and refuge and salvation, a private life of his own choice and after his own human heart. The five hundred million should allow him this; nay more, they should insist

in their own interests that he has it. If it happens
to be with the Invaders, *tant pis*. . . .

Shock brigade of the gossips, real sin-scenters have
been busy too. Over one aspect of the King's life
they have succeeded in raising a doubt.

The doubt is: Where should the line be drawn
between his elementary indefeasible rights and freedom as a human being and his duty and dignity as
England's most precious public institution? Wedded
to duty (and to No Other), proudly and humbly
aware of his unique position and its unique obligations
as he is, King Edward would yet draw a line leaving
the small area of his personal freedom a little less
small than some subjects fancy.

These, the disapprovers, are unfortunately not
only muck-rakers, pinched Puritans, Yankee-baiters,
not only snubbed snobs and despited duchesses
seeking to get even with him for his known coolness
towards the old nobles and preference for the
common herd, and common Americans. They
include many to whom the King as sign of the greatness and goodness of England is their chief political
ideal. They include many of the great loyalist middle
class. They include almost all *who know*.

It has paradoxical aspects, this King-tattle. Moral
enthusiasm keeps it alive, even more than immoral.
By a convention (that helps the country a little, but
the King less), it is kept out of print; elsewhere it
rages, without respect to decency and perhaps

probability. It is trivial to a degree, and yet holds a hint of drama, even of tragedy; because, however *remote* certain of the possibilities it criminally toys with, these would be tremendous and England-shaking if Fate turned them into fact.

Some of us are not among the disapprovers. We think that a King, we think that Edward, has a right to the scant private happiness he can find; we think that, if the pursuit of that happiness does not, as in his case it does not, affect—except favourably—unselfish devotion to public duty in any manner or degree whatsoever, he should be left for pity's sake, and gratitude's, in peace.

And yet——. And yet, Your Majesty—Your strange mighty role is vicarious; it is expiatory; it is ideal. Very humbly we (the not-disapprovers) pray you: Cross-examine your secret conscience once again, and if its answer should reveal—as we do not believe it need reveal—the faintest shadow of conflict between your pleasure as man and your pains as king, then—hard and cheerless though it should be, decide (dutifully we beg you) in favour of the latter; and England.

After Edward, will it last?

As far as his heirs decide the matter, no evident reason why not.

Duke of York, next heir, would make a good and popular king in the sound tradition of his father.

Then come York's small daughters. Well, in England
we don't mind queens.

> *"It's a gent! It's a gent!"*
> *Crowed the Duchess of Kent.*
> *"Oh, bother the stork!"*
> *Sighed the Duchess of York.*

Sighs superfluous. In England we don't mind
queens.

Apart, possibly, from the writing of novels, the
one field of public endeavour open to both sexes in
which women have proved themselves the equals,
at least the equals, of men is the exercise of personal
sovereignty. In proportion, there have been more
great queens than kings.

Nitocris, *Khnem Amen*, Cleopatra; Semiramis,
Tomyris; Artemisia Queen of Halicarnassus, Artemisia
Queen of Caria. Dido Queen of Carthage; Zenobia
Queen of Palmyra; Athaliah Queen of Judah. The
great Japanese empresses who throve in regnant splen-
dour during our Dark Ages; their contemporary
sisters of Byzantium—the terrible Theodoras, Irenes
and Zoës, with Empress Ariadne, Empress Eudoxia,
Empress Anne. Isabella of Castile, Mary Queen of
Scots, Catherine de' Medici; Christine of Sweden,
Maria Theresa, Catherine the Great. Ranavalona I;
Ranavalona II, Ranavalona III. Liliuokalani the Last;
Queen of the Sandwich Isles. Tsze-Hsi, that bad old

Boxer who as a little girl had been laid naked for the Emperor in the Chamber of Divine Repose, and advanced from a first mistress's bed to be the last master of the Middle Kingdom. . . .

The little ladies of 145 Piccadilly may not, as yet, bear much resemblance to some of these distinguished princesses of the past: our own English history is good augury enough for women sovereigns. The three great periods of English history are the Elizabethan, the Age of Good Queen Anne, the Victorian.

The English people—English men, with their highly developed faculty for the idealization of women—would take a curious sentimental satisfaction in, and have a new depth of chivalrous loyalty ready for, the accession of a female ruler. A queen would be rapturously welcomed. This psychological verity (vainly darkened by those who, rather prematurely, summon up the spectre of another Prince Consort) seems to be overlooked by the meddlers in his private affairs who, not without a good argument or two, would push His Majesty into matrimony. They do not realize how many of their fellow-subjects would, however respectfully, feel half sorry at such an event, however auspicious. It might deprive us of Elizabeth II.

The young heiress-presumptive, at ten years old, has already in her face and bearing the makings of an adequate successor, with no imaginative doubts or self-doubts whatsoever, to that most high and mightye

Princesse dread Sovereign Lady Elizabeth, by the Grace of God Queene of England, France and Irelande, Defender of the trewe ancient and Catholic faith, most worthy Empresse from the Orcade Isles to the Montaynes Pyrenei. Next on the list, her little sister looks attractive. Both will be trained perfectly for their portentous possible job.

Whichever of them all it may one day be, there is no single sinister figure on the whole Windsor horizon.

Even so:

Even if there be no danger to this Crown from the personalities and probabilities of this Family; if from politics, powers and parties the danger is inconsiderable; if from the divers unfavouring tendencies —frivolity and instability of the age, its not decreasing indifference to national needs and national tradition; plutocracy, Press; moral defeatism, political salvationism, bolshevism, fascism—it may still emerge immune: even so, in history one may not prophesy the probable. In '14 who so wise (who so crazy) as to foretell that in four brief years the four Emperors of Europe would not be; or, in '24, that a long forgotten form of government like dictatorship would by '34 have re-appeared in wide triumph?

There are enormous imponderables. The ill state of man in general, and his soul and mind in this hour. The woes these may bring. War; world

revolution; world absolute madness; world collapse
and chaos.

The King may vanish to-night; or live for ever.
He is very fragile, and very strong.

If he stays, he well may lose political power and the
political aspect altogether, to be solely the Symbol.

Or his power may increase.

The new inventions and tendencies have increased
the likelihood of personal types of government, and
their strength. Photography, cinematography, the
popular Press, the wireless, have enabled the One
Man to impress his personality upon multitudes as
never in the history of the great nation-states before.
Elected chambers and unelected civil services, however ambitious or powerful, can make no such
effective use of the image, the broadcast voice. The
revived sense of history, and of hero-worship; the
subjective need, frustrated under the rationalist
democracies (plutocracies, bureaucracies), for rule
and a sign of rule more concrete and individual than
anything that assemblies or officials can offer, for a
seen ruling reality above the unrealities of administrative anonymity; the objective need, in a world
ever more wayward and more complicated, for
Authority; the returned belief that at one place of
government, the top, the One can do better than
the many:—these things, and others, all conspire
towards a revival of monarchy. So far, and elsewhere,

it is the new dictators who have benefited. Here, in maturer England, it is possible that within English limits it may be the ancient King. With not less advantage to his people, and less chance of the disadvantages: the denial of feasible liberty, the war-mongering, cruelty, hate, horror.

His theoretical powers are still there, intact. The letter of the law still vests in him vastest authority. Such a change could come without upset.

He, and we, may one day have need of those powers: to fight other powers, irresponsible powers of wealth or wildness. Exercised in a great crisis, in the interests of the mass of the nation against an extreme faction, strong only by money or violence, they would find the mass of the nation upholding them.

It is extreme factions, only, who fear the King. Those who desire ultimate upheaval—not the great social amelioration which, certainly, can be obtained within our present system, peacefully—who seek Soviet with themselves as its masters, and as tyrants (Secret Police State) over the rest of the people; those are afraid that the despised half-moribund monarchy might stand in their way. It might. As it might be our equal salvation against the black opposite brand of tyranny, which the other extremists (so unlike, so like) would be paving the way for. The personal element in rule could, in England, prove our protection against that kind of personal rule which we, England, are most hostile to.

It may go differently. Enough of the old doctrinaire anti-king sentiment may support the extremists, black or red, to help them win and beat the king. Or he himself may misjudge, or misuse; assume a party issue to be a national one; take sides; the wrong side. The first time Labour comes in with a clear Labour majority and a true Labour programme, there are some who foresee—a tiny few who hope for—the clash. Labour brings in some bill that the rich, the middle classes, and everyone else but Labour bitterly dislikes. The Lords reject it. Labour brings in its bill to abolish the Lords. The King, believing that 'the country' is with him, supports his co-hereditaries, and summons Madam Veto from her long sleep. He refuses his assent: then Labour. . . .

Whether his power increases or declines, in the magian era ahead his emblematic and mysterious value will grow. He will wear his Crown more often.

He will wear it in Durbar. He will wear it in each Dominion. If the Empire survives—and the Crown helps it to—the Crown Imperial it will ever more clearly become. The King's role as Head of the allied British peoples will gain upon his ancient and local role as ruler of England; the Emperor will gain upon the King. England will be no more than the doyen of his kingdoms, his headquarters rather than his home.

· · · · · · ·

The job, the fantastic tremendous position, the high headship of five hundred million people, Emperor-King, *Idol* of one fourth of the earth, is almost intolerable.

Be tolerant therefore.

Spare carping, and cackle. Shew mercy. Shew justice. Approve the large merit of his public life; cease probing into his small corner of private life.

Simply wish him well. Except for the dearest of my family and the nearest of my friends, I wish more good to Edward than to any other being in the world.

ABDICATION

I

A few weeks later.

THE King of England wished to do a thing it was not possible for him, as King of England, to do. The Prime Minister of England, duly and correctly in his function, told the King it was not possible. The King, correct in his function, took his Prime Minister's word for it.

He said: "I am prepared to go."

I said: "Sir, that is grievous news."

He had a choice. Between doing what he wished, and staying King of England; which also he may have wished.

He chose.

He chose to go.

Through the criss-cross and confusion of all the theories, guesses, lies, libels, doubts, sympathies, side-issues, that looks to be the main thread, not disputed; amid the fancies, the one unalloyed Fact.

It is, however interesting, strictly irrelevant that those who would have had the King do as he desired to do may have formed a very large minority of his subjects. That they may even—there are no means

255

of knowing, one way or the other—have been the majority. That they may even also, by a majority of standards, have been right.

This only is relevant: that the people on the other side, those who were against the King's project—the almost unanimity of the responsible people, the decisive people and the *rulers* in both England and Dominions, with the evident bulk of the middle class and, at the least, large numbers of the poorer classes also, the ruled—together constituted a body of opinion so formidable that it could in any circumstances have prevented, as so very easily it did prevent, the realization of the project. Against that mighty opposition *it was not possible for him* to carry his point.

I think the opponents had the advantage, too, that they felt more strongly against the project than the King's supporters did in its favour. The latter were merely in favour of the King's right to do as he wanted; scarcely ever in favour of his plan for its own sake. Which, on much stronger ground, was what the opponents opposed.

If our Fact is assailable, it is from a quite different angle.

"Yes, as things in the end did happen, were manœuvred to happen, Edward no doubt could not have brought it off. But the heart, rotten heart, of the matter is those manœuvrings, by means of which your supposedly straight and central fact was artfully shaped into one. Many very dubious questions have to be answered, dubious lips unsealed . . ."

Whether the Prime Minister found his historic task easier to perform because of personal or political or puritanical disapproval of the Other. Whether there was any such disapproval. Whether, if the King had been a safer National Government king—had not been impatient with the Cabinet's policy, lack of policy, for the Distressed Areas and unemployment and poverty, had not been against the Means Test and known to be, and generally a nasty little Bolshie (or Fascist, when that came handier) who privately preferred the masses to the classes and say Mr. Kirkwood to Mr. Baldwin—the latter might not have made efforts *that would have succeeded* somehow to forestall and prevent what befell. Whether things might not have been managed a bit better; or very much worse. (Picture a Labour Government in at the time. No Baldwin. Work it out.) Whether, faced earlier, and the Press freed earlier, the affair might not have had a pleasanter outcome; or the same outcome; or an unpleasanter, whether Madam Veto was but Mrs. Grundy, and the denial of the King's desire was earnest of the narrowness and nationalism, priggishness and prudishness, of the British peoples; or of their soundness, sure instinct and high sense of decency and destiny. Whether Edward ought not to have preferred his duty to his desire, sacrificed himself Man to himself Thing, one form of Eternity to

257

another form of Eternity; or whether he shewed himself braver, and truer alike to the human heart's highest values and the Crown's own dignity, in not so doing. Whether these dilemmas and alternatives are the real ones; or others, going deeper, that no one yet has put . . .

Whether Baldwin and Company did not *plant* (both senses) King Edward before a terrible dilemma they would never have brought a king after their own heart to face?

No one, yet—or perhaps ever—can answer these questions.

Truth is complicated. Truth is elusive.

Impute however the worst to 'Baldwin and the bishops.' The worst that, on evidence not prejudice, seems at all likely is this: First that they did not make the same allowances and efforts as they would have made for a king they had liked better, personally and politically. Second, that once battle was joined they used every art (the means and moment of publicity, and so forth) swiftly to secure victory for their point of view—the point of view, they believed, of the country's history and Empire's safety—and discreetly to discredit a King who, they believed, was bringing his great office and the State into mortal danger.

Even so: they did not provoke, if naturally they neither damped nor tactically discouraged, the great uprising of opinion which echoed their own "Thumbs down!" and declared Edward's desire undesirable. Still less did they 'frame' him into desiring it.

Is it so sure?

There are several theories. That Edward's resolution to marry was his own. Or her own.

That on the contrary he was quite content with the position as it was until others put into his head, insinuated to him (weak, chivalrous, suggestionable) that he *ought* to marry her. That those others were of the Favourite's own set, the fast night-club Americans and half and pseudo-Americans, who pushed her on, and him on, in the cause of their own ascension; as in regal France two centuries ago the Pâris brothers and the *vivriers* pushed the Pompadour, and d'Aiguillon and the *viveurs* pushed the du Barry.

That those Others—the 'Americans' unconsciously working with them, to be dished as usual in the end by the artfuller English—were *agents provocateurs* of the aristocrats and reactionaries. "As mistress—if she is one—we can't do so very much against her, or him; but let us get it into his obstinate little head that it is his duty to marry her and then we have him; fixed; finished."

It is a serious accusation.

With on the whole insufficient evidence, so far, to support it. *Cui bono?* of course. . .

Endless evidence, on the other hand, and persuasive, and very nearly convincing, in support of the ortho-dox or official story:—that Baldwin played his cards cutely but played them straight, or fairly straight; knew his own mind, and that the great mass of responsible people who cared for the Crown, here and overseas, was of the same mind; knew the King, and his mind, and so feared that the issue could not be evaded; honestly yet hoped—this decidedly less certain, and rather less important—that the King would make the choice he did not make.

I, who liked Edward but not so much the others, believe that the desire and the determination were his own; that, given more time and every opportunity, he probably would not have forgone them; that even if he, instead of the others, could have chosen the moment and means of making them known to people and Empire, the sentiment against them would have been scarcely less.

No, say diehard Windsormen: If silence had been broken earlier, Edward would still be King. He would have seen—what he did not see until too late—that his plan was not feasible, and so would never have brought himself and the Monarchy into the humiliating position they tricked him into. The villains of the piece are those who imposed secrecy, well aware that it must be fatal.

This, like some other Machiavellian versions, is not altogether easy to swallow; at any rate neat. Clearly the matter should never have been allowed to get so far; but that it was so allowed may be proof less of Baldwin's guilt than of his lack of guile, less of his knavery than of his deficiency in tact and worldly-wisdom—for the abundance of which he has been so warmly praised, and self-praised.

Perhaps deservedly. Who knows?

Who knows anything?

In all the Affair, obscure points are the great majority.

Remember that when cleared up, if ever, most of them may turn out less favourable to Edward's case than to "Baldwin's."

If, of those two ferocious campaigns of opposing calumny, Anti-King was the more effective, that may among other causes have been because its inspiration was drawn more largely—less rarely—at the source of truth.

Nearly all versions current assume some measure of conflict, at least latent, between monarch and minister. It is quite unproved that there was any. Nobody knows: except the high few who do. The whole affair may have been arranged beforehand, as between friends, and the Prime Minister's timing of secrecy and sudden publicity a piece of long-range subtlety, which the peaceful outcome abundantly justified. There may have been no ill-feeling. None of that shouting and swearing. One may really have said of the other, as an edifying minority-story has it: "Thank God I had good old S.B. with me through it all."

Both sides, some say, were playing for position. Baldwin stacking the pack, the King popularity-hunting. Baldwin played better. If, as alleged, he was hard at it compiling the King's *dossier*, the King played into his hands by supplying him with generous material. "You may bet," ran the most triumphant of all the Whispers, "that there's more to it than old Baldwin chooses to say. He would never be taking so strong a line unless there were *other* things . . ."

Unfortunately there were.

Things done and said in his infatuation; his lover's prodigality; his shrill King's rage against those who denied her to him. In moments of recourse to other sources of courage as well. In hours of erratic, or erotic, obstinacy. Things left undone, in his in-fatuation. Duty neglected. Papers held up. Papers curiously, neo-Kaiserishly, annotated. The affair of the Egyptian Treaty. No sound understanding of the technique, or limitations, or necessary dignity of the office. Irregular hours; irregular habits. Muddling. Fuddling. Meddling . . .

Aspects of Ipswich.

The day with Ataturk. The day in Athens. The day in Aberdeen.

That Deeside engagement was of long standing, and the Silver City had decked herself not frugally to greet him. At the last moment he deputed Duke and Duchess to open the Infirmary and carry out all his programme; then himself drove from Balmoral into the city not to do his duty but to meet a band of gay Transatlantics at the station. That night, on the dour granite walls, "Down with the American whore!" was chalked up. As for Lola; as for the du Barry. It was indeed the Writing on the Wall.

There followed the yet greater crime of his visit to desolate Wales; *The Times* rumbled; and his doom was sealed.

Reflect a moment, to yourself, on the various cruelty and wickedness of this world.

Then will it seem a poor little list of crimes to have broken an adored and devoted King for; that, and being in love.

'Dereliction of duty' (at the very end, once or twice, triflingly, in the gathering anguish of his fight against them) there may have been—how hoped for, how pounced upon! Was it no dereliction of duty complacently to leave half England derelict?

Contempt of the necessary dignity of his office meant evasion of certain excesses of Court etiquette. Irregular hours meant having once kept the Right Honourable Jack in Office waiting for five minutes. Meddling meant trying to help the unfortunate.

They hated him, without a doubt. His marriage plan was their pretext perfect.

Whether or no they invented, Lord how they welcomed her!

In wanting to get rid of him for his other misdeeds, they may have been wrong; they may very well have been right. But until this marriage was mooted, they had no notion *how* to get rid of him.

She, whom they pretended was a disaster, was in fact a godsend. Her two divorces were a gift from Heaven. Without them, an excuse good enough might have been damned difficult to find. They should not be reviling her. They should be setting up statues in her honour.

A hunted creature he had always been; an Orphan, face and soul, for ever. And now they had gotten him in a corner, *trapped*.

Puzzled, dimly, he yet had managed to feel, through childhood, princehood, now brief kinghood, all the things that he had had to be, the strange things "they" (we) wanted and pretended him to be: ruler, symbol, ideal, idol, good sort, priest, good sport, talisman, gentleman, tailor's block, commercial traveller, son and lover, hero, god. . . . He had played each part to the best of his ability and high courage, to the wide limits of his powers of physical and moral endurance.

Nervous endurance was the rub. To go on, he had to have ever more stimulus, more freedom from godhead (the bores, the bowing), more contrast.

264

He had no Friends. He had no intellectual or spiritual resources. Rest he was incapable of. Violent exercise was, after his thirties, not stimulus enough.

At last he had found it, an elixir of courage and continuance—an ever-new transfusion of vitality—in the company, and adoration, of a set of fast Transatlantic wise-crackers.

He may have found there, among them, in the end, something better than a drug; deserving another, diviner, name.

Whichsoever it was, healing medicine or hopeless stimulant, after a while he could not keep going and play the Part without a dose, an injection, every day or two; then every few hours.

"Before, ninety per cent of the time I was unhappy, ten per cent happy. Now I am ten per cent unhappy, ninety per cent happy."

Happy?

Pictures did not shew it. That last year or two the retarded adolescent face, the tragic eyes, did not reveal it. The loveliness almost gone, the look of a debauched lost boy came over it instead; with an *increase*, if possible, of the misery. I don't know.

Anyway, he had found or believed he had found the means (beauty or poison) of strength for his task; the means he must for ever have by him if he were to go on performing his great task. So he the KING-

265   s

EMPEROR, lord of a fourth of the world, humbly asked for the means to be made his, honourably and perpetually available.

They said *No*.

It was a hard cruel blow in the face.

Unexpected, apparently. The wisecrackers had told him he could bring it off. These were the only people he talked to intimately; aliens who knew even less than they cared of the English, and their morality and history, their pride and prejudice.

With all his social sympathies, and personal sympathy and flair, he was not much more in touch with his people's soberer ideals, or their deep traditional side, than the aliens were. His continual travelling had prevented his establishing a steady contact with steady opinion anywhere. Apparently he himself thought he would bring it off.

He found arguments that impressed him. Better blood than some ugly German princessling. Better than a political match, with continental complications. Better for Anglo-American relations. Better to marry for love.

Impressed him, but not them. 'Moral' issues they now mumbled of.

But it is because I am moral that I want to marry her. If I don't marry her, I'm attacked as immoral and those parsons won't give me communion, coronation. If I want to marry her, I'm not allowed.

If I defy them and do—still those priests won't give me their communion, coronation.

Obstinate, knowing it was for duty's sake he needed it, desperately needing it, King-Emperor—he persisted.

It is unreasonable; it is bitterly unfair. Why shhuld I, the King of England, alone in England be treated so, and not be free to marry the Woman I Love?

He misargued there. How many of the King's subjects can easily marry outside their caste, or colour, or convention? In nearly all countries the humblest diplomat, being a representative person, must ask his Government's permission to marry the lady of his choice; not rarely refused. It is not unreasonable, it is more reasonable, that the chief Representative Person of the chief empire of the earth should have his freedom of choice limited somewhat.

No doubt Henry VIII could marry whom, and as often as, he liked. Bloody Mary his daughter defied Parliament and bitter feeling in the country, and dragged Philip of Spain into her barren bed. But they were another *sort* of king: masters not symbols. The old mystery-king, which ours has become again, could no more have acted so than Edward VIII could.

Even in that age, its greatest sovereign set an example. While the Queen of Scots sacrificed always the interests of her country to her woman's love, the Queen of England subordinated every private passion she had to the good of the State. One lives in every Englishman's political memory, and his pride and gratitude, as his greatest sovereign; the other in the whole world's heart as a lover.

As Edward will live.

When however *political* England drummed "Duty, duty! Sacrifice, sacrifice!" into his weary ears, she was not wrong.

Nor he. There are different planes of duty, and sacrifice; and reality, and eternity.

Anyway, they had him in the trap. Give her up or go! That great tragic struggle between Love and Duty began.

I wonder if there was any such struggle. I think the tragedy may have been that there was no struggle; that he knew he *could not* live without the thing that kept him afloat, and so had no choice. He knew beforehand which alternative he must choose; which alternative from before birth had been chosen for him.

That made it no happier.

If ever kingship was *representative*, it was now. Here were private emotions, primitive, romantic, authentic; with the added sense of public issues hanging upon them; and lived in public, for the subjects to see, share and live for themselves. The subjects were excitedly half-happy. He was not.

It was high historic drama, played before us.

There were moments of melodrama, of light comedy, farce even; of pure drama chiefly, with tragedy. There were laughs, and low places; the heights were Æschylean.

The scene laid in kings' palaces; in Majesty's hidden retreat from which, from every window, lights blazed out into the December night; in kings' hearts. The comings and goings of the great. Brief appearances, trivial yet (who knew?) fateful, of absurdly unimportant—during those hours absurdly important—personages: clerks, courtiers, Royal Dukes, lackeys. The two Women of the play, so ominously different; one, the One, at last secretly flying by night over the sea and zigzag across France, Hollywood fashion and by Hollywood pursued. The two Men, as contrasted in body, soul and mind as two beings of the same race and sex could be. The one's nights of anguish without sleep; the other's days of tremendous historic responsibility. The scenes of lost anger and grim calm, human pleading and high political obduracy that they had— that we imagined them having—together. The chances, the changes. Hope, fear, conjecture, strain; sympathy and pure sorrow; awful pleasure. The audience, the people of the British Empire, wavered for one first staggering minute; then turned actor, took the stage and, conscious of ancient genius, took the lead.

Grave emotions, and the victorious political ones,

never for more than a moment wholly excluded pleasurable ones from this Chief Actor's breast. He savoured them at street corners, in factory, boudoir, club, pub, around moral middle-class breakfast table. The thrill it was, the dark delicious excitement; with spice of danger and destiny. Gossip—Have you heard this one?—in quantity and quality such as never had been, and about royal Majesty. No President could give such money's worth as this. The joy of freely airing one's low prejudices, or one's high freedom from them, on a perfect subject that gave fullest play to either.

Among the country's reasons against the Marriage, the least was the 'American' reason. It was not a reason at all. For an English marriage of the same stripe would have been equally impossible. And *an* American marriage would have been possible. Only not this one.

The Invaders, of course, were not beloved. They were as a rule no credit to the great country they had exploited and deserted nor to the one in which they now were roystering and ruling. Enormous fortunes, doubtfully acquired, had for a generation been heightening the pace and lowering the tone of English society. Their money could apparently buy everything:—old houses, old names (there were 'old' families in the peerage three-quarters rich-American, and new families four-quarters), old

decencies, the greatest of our newspapers, the chief
places in society and the public eye. Their accent
was beginning to be an asset, even to the English
themselves, in truly 'smart' circles. It was beginning
—you listened in, that night?—to be heard in the
voice of the young tribal God himself. . . . They
were cock-a-hoop, and since Edward's accession
getting insolent and quite out-of-hand. There was
but one more world to conquer. The first woman to
sit in the ancient Commons was a divorced American;
why not then also——?

Being without rank or title was no reason.

Although not very many were aware of the kind of
society this union would have brought to the top,
their knowledge was decisive. It hardened the
opposition of those among them who would have
opposed anyhow, or who had personally suffered
from the insolence or interference of the new
Gavestonne; far more important, it decided the
feelings of liberal people who, on principle, would
have liked the King free to choose, and have preferred
a democratic marriage. Anything more undemocratic than that foreign band of plutocratic pleasure-
seekers was not conceivable, nor more harmful to the
dignity and national character of the throne. Some of
the most contemptible people alive, and that their
native country had scornfully spewed forth, were
closest around our King. Left-wing opinion—loose
fish aside—which knew anything of that circle where

he had fixed his choice was as unfavourable as the frowstiest 'duchess.'

The moral and sacramental objections to divorce had some weight; how much weight it is very difficult to guess.

The chief, nearly the whole, reason was this:—for Queen of England an itinerant shop-soiled twice-divorcée with two ex-husbands living was *not good enough*.

She came too far below, she clashed too crudely, with the nation's idea and ideal, dream and myth, of feminine royalty. Queen Elizabeth, Queen Victoria; Queen Alexandra, Queen Mary; the ladies of York, Gloucester, Kent: whichever standard among these variant high ones, of English queenship your own might happen to be, the new aspirant did not fit it. Ideals are ideals. Idols must be idols. She *would not do*. The come-down from Queen Mary to Queen Wally was too steep.

Strong at the outset, these sentiments gathered strength hourly. Between the two meetings of Parliament, over that week-end 4th to 8th, they became a torrent. You could see the beautiful surface-wave, King, subsiding; feel the powerful groundswell, Crown and Country, rising up.

For the King still held: his personality; the love for him, as real in many hearts as ever was for a royal man. Gratitude for those twenty-five years of great

Prince-of-Wales-hood. The fact of being King: the antique sentiment of personal loyalty; the deep, rather perhaps than wide, sentiment that He was sacred, and required more reverent handling. The feeling that he deserved at least more human handling; sympathy with a young man at bay being bullied and badgered by a lot of smarmy self-righteous old men.

The other side gathered far more strength, and prevailed.

Partly it was that first emotions, proving their soundness on reflection, grew stronger. Partly that human nature is generous first, critical after.

Members of Parliament came back from Sabbaths in their constituencies, in west, Wales, north, Scotland; places with a different notion of national dignity from Piccadilly's.

Labour and the Left overcame their first doubt, and although their generous people had a regard for the King and knew that he had more genuine under-dog sympathies than any king there had ever been or than they were ever again likely to get, they chose to follow head not heart. In the difference between King and Minister which was made known to them by the latter, and the death-struggle between King and Parliament which can only have been made known to them by special revelation, they instinctively ranged themselves against the royal side. Where Puritanism also placed them. Where Cabinet propaganda that the King was a 'Fascist' helped to place them.

England is proud, and minded seeing her Throne provide a music-hall turn for low foreign newspapers. Hearst's role was suspect. The country bitterly resented the other country's brazen delighted cheapening of its high possession—the tabloid press jeering, interfering—and in its anger naturally, if ungratefully, ignored the correct and cordial tone of most Americans and of the good American journals. (On balance, there has in all this affair been quite as much unjustified abuse of America by England as of England by America. The latter, under provocation, and temptation, has behaved on the whole extremely well.)

Those who came out as King's champions were an unprepossessing company. An unstable ambitious politician, flitter from party to party, extreme reactionary, himself the first-fruit of the first famous snob-dollar marriage; 'half an alien and wholly undesirable,' as long ago was said. An unstable ambitious politician, flitter from party to party, extreme reactionary, whose wife had been the fruit of another eminent snob-dollar marriage; leader of a movement in spirit wholly alien and wholly undesirable, as some dare think. A prominent divorcé. Foreigners. Lord Rotherbrook. Lord Beavermere. A highbrow writer or two, famous loose livers. Bernard Shaw, buffooning; ever since on the wrong

side of seventy, always on the wrong side politically.
There was something in what he said. But not nearly
enough.

Millions of poor people, tolerant simple people,
devoted to Edward, formed a romantic King's Party
in the country. But these—foreigners, half-
foreigners, doubtful cards (morally, politically),
Fascists, flashists, press lords—were its 'leaders.'

King's Party talk only harmed the King, who had
done nothing to promote it. Because a bare hint of
personal rule alarms us. Because he is King of the
nation, not any party; least of all one of his own.

There were the newspaper accounts of luxury
and frivolity; the photographs; the sudden revelation, realization how an un-English set of
noceurs—we gradually got some of their names and
hard faces—had cornered the King. No sovereign of
England, not George I with his Hanoverians, had
been so wrapped up in foreigners since Henry III and
his Poitevins and Savoyards. In preferring their
company and ways the King had failed in a chief duty:
his duty as representative chief of his own nation.

He had come short yet more signally in harbouring
a plan that troubled the nation, that was unacceptable
to the more national-minded part of the nation, that
raised deep dividing issues of morals and conduct and
dignity which the King, our arch-unifier, alone in
England should never raise.

Much of those days' exciting news was evidently

based on fact. The rapacity, the vulgarity. What was not so evidently based did also its bit: the rumour and hearsay, fantastic, orgiastic—spies, crimes, vice, Hitler—never surpassed in the rich long history of scandal-mongering. Whether they were wholly true, or wholly untrue, or something in between, those stories heaped—already half in revenge—upon the head of a woman unable to defend herself sealed finally her fate. If such stories—true or not, *no matter* —were in circulation about you, you were not fit to be Queen of England.

It is not known that she wanted to.

The throne's prestige was being harmed by all the publicity, vulgarity. By the delay. Time was being lost, business held up; many a mug-manufacturer was losing money. The country's public business was being held up. The foreign situation was troubled; uncertainty had gone on quite long enough. He had had quite time enough to make up his mind. It was not decent to be so carefully weighing a private preference against the world's supreme historic dignity and duty. A King must not rate his personal sentiments *too* high. A base rumour was set going, to break him finally, that Edward himself was prolonging the crisis holding out for more money. . . .

After the gamut of the emotions had been passed through; after that unique week of excitement, dignity and foulness; of high tone, for the world to see, in Parliament (but low in the lobbies)—by the eve of abdication sympathy with the King had measurably dwindled, and support for the Government immeasurably grown.

There were three broad divisions of opinion.

Against abdication, whatever the outcome. Against Edward, *hoping* abdication would be the outcome. And, third, those who desired Edward but who believed that the marriage would endanger the Crown which is greater even than King, and that in face of the opposition it was in any case not possible; and who ranged themselves therefore, with private sorrow often, with political hesitation hardly, on the side of the Government and of Mr., and Mrs., Baldwin.

I estimate the third group to have been the largest, and the second and third groups combined much larger than the first.

King Edward so estimated, and so went.

You said: We loved him, and we have let him down. Or: We thought he loved us, and he has let us down.

Three set speeches were the Shakespearean curtain. What did you think of them?

Each man and woman thought different.

And so in the future men and women will think. Therefore there will never be, on any of these strange events, any grey prevailing judgment that is 'History'; but black and white always, a pitched battle of absolutes, as over Mary Stuart or Charles

277

Stuart and all the great persons and passions of the world's story.

The archbishop's? What was it: a cynical jest, a blasphemous leg-pull—the head of a church founded on the rock, not of Peter, but of a sordid divorce case now highfalutin about morals far less sordid? (*Kick him, he's down!* is no precept of the Mount). Or, not rather, a deserved and dignified rebuke—if anything too mild and Christian a rebuke, given the enormity of their offence—from the historic head of the national religion and morality to a band of raffish ne'er-do-wells who had ruined our king, sent him away broken, and risked our kingship?

The Prime Minister's? One of the most interesting speeches, matter and manner, Mother of Parliaments has ever heard, one of the most masterly. Did you yet scent a faint faint flavour of casuistry, jesuitry, cunning with simple, meek triumph amid the tears: pure Baldwin? Or was it the effort, seeking no effects, of an honest great Englishman, worn out after being for a fateful week England, telling with sincere emotion plain truth?

What is truth?

And Prince Edward's: the leave-taking listened to by more human beings than any utterance before in the world, and to be remembered when all the other utterances of this age are long forgotten? Did it move you to tears, or sneers, or . . .

.　　　.　　　.　　　.　　　.

278

He left his land with kingly dignity; he repaired to the welcomer company of rich American Jewesses holding almost world records for divorce. We saw him go with love, and pity; and cynical relief. Was it so heartless of those South Wales film audiences, unemployed, entrance half-price, stonily not to cheer him? He was a tragic, broken man; but he was off to the sun, and the white snow, with full trunks and full pockets, and they——

II

My own small crisis within the crisis was What to do with this book?

The very day Bradford put match to the powder barrel I had put the last touch to the chapter 'Edward VIII.'

December Days over, I thought the thing could stand. Except for part of that Edward chapter and, more elusively, here and there for the *tone* of the book, written in the spirit of his reign, it seemed that most of what I had written was still apposite; and some of it more apposite than before.

Apposite because, in every essential, things are unchanged.

No change in the power, or the position, or permanently the prestige of the Crown. No new departures dynastic, or political, or constitutional.

No real change in the public opinion in favour of the monarchy, or in the parliamentary relation to it.

As you were.

Especially as you were before January, 1936. Seems more than a twelvemonth since Old George died. God, what he'd have said! . . .

Some points were confirmed, or made clearer. It was seen that the King still had the faculty of changing his Prime Minister. If opinion in Parliament and the country had been much less strongly against the marriage, but the Cabinet no less strongly than it actually was, the King could, and with wide approval probably would, have sent for another statesman to form an alternative Government. It was seen, on the other hand, that so seemingly private an affair as the monarch's matrimonial intentions was a public question, for Cabinet advice; which the King must take, or seek advice elsewhere. A Symbol King's espousals are more important than his politics.

The immense passionate obsessional interest of this nation in the Throne was seen clearer than ever.

The more solemn constitutional conclusions that were drawn registered also, if they registered anything, confirmation rather than change.

"The constitutional crisis has demonstrated the essential soundness of the British Constitution." "The supremacy of Parliament triumphantly affirmed itself in answer to the challenge."

There is no British Constitution. There was no constitutional crisis. Edward acted so as to prevent the shadow of one arising. One never arose. There was only the personal crisis. Nobody challenged Parliament's supremacy. Parliament was never consulted on the affair. Our two kings handled it privately together. Edward's case was impossible, so the case was no test. It was because Parliament represented (if over-represented) the nation's view that the King's case was impossible that it had so easy a victory; or rather no victory, because it received no challenge.

Had the pieces been placed on the board only a little differently; had King's desire been, instead of impossible, merely of rather difficult acceptance—say one ex-husband instead of two, and he in Paradise—then the supremacy of Parliament, in the sense suggested, would have counted for no more than Blunt's grunts or the ire of the unctuous archbishops. As the pieces lay, Parliament and the prelates were on the same side as the people: and the possible. Which is why they prevailed.

Parliament behaved well. The weakness of her would-be rivals, Communism and Fascism, stood out. All the British Parliaments behaved well. The Australian debate was the best. The Canberra speeches were the most interesting, and the most independent, that were made anywhere. Read them.

Fortunate that the issue *was* so clear-cut. If King's

desire had been of some awkward intermediate
suitability, there would have been a cleavage of
responsible opinion. Then there would have been a
crisis. As things were—and will be, for poetry not
politics will always have first claim on the tale—
there was only the human disaster.

The No Change view is not everywhere held.

Some think that the Monarchy has taken a very bad
knock.

That chatter has cheapened and serious talk
seriously weakened it.

That it is no longer taken for granted.

At this hour of the story of the world it is a matter
for ridicule that two grown-up men should spend
long days of the public time solemnly debating the
amorous affairs of one of them. And ridicule kills.

The *uselessness* of the Idol and Mummer was never
so clearly shewn up: and in the very roles we retain
him for, the representative and the imperial role.
It was the Minister, not the Mummer, who represented public opinion, the public emotion and conscience, *as against* the Mummer paid and exalted to
do so. It was the Minister who treated with the
Dominions, and stood for their point of view as for
ours. Imperial Link did poorly. It simply did not
function. Instead, the Prime Minister of England
functioned. Statute of Westminster which, the books
said, would secure the Dominions direct access to the

Crown secured the exact opposite: access to the English Prime Minister alone, and that at a test moment when the latter was in conflict with the Crown. Virtually alone. Dominion dealings with Fort Belvedere were formal, and based on Downing Street's presentation of the case.

In that way, in every way, the crisis shewed the superfluity of the King, the almightiness and national and imperial function of the Minister. Baldwin that week was King-Emperor.

The hereditary principle has been shaken.

First, because—for all to see—it provided us with so unsuitable a Chief. A man who disliked glory and ceremony, who undervalued dignity and tradition, and who paid no body or even lip service to bourgeois morality either, was a man who (whatever his other good points, or secret goodness) had too slender a basis of support to succeed as English King. You can't run an ancient monarchy on "saxophone and cocktail-party" lines. Yet the man who tried to was one whom tradition and training had together produced; a man who (whatever the pathos of him) put himself before his job, insisted on ways that were wayward, and persisted in a project from which alike public spirit and private altruism, good judgement and common sense should have dissuaded him.

Second, in that, by dismissing Edward in favour of George, we have been taking a step back towards the

Anglo-Saxon elected kingship. Rejecting primo-
geniture, the nation again has been *choosing*, as of old,
that member of the kingly family which it thinks best
fitted to be its king.

Within strict limits, this is true; within very strict
limits indeed, perhaps good.

Still, there was danger, of more sorts than one, in
changing over.

'Why don't they take the Duke of Kent?'

Why not? But if we could start picking and
choosing within the Family, why not without it?

Why not? . . .

The one undisputed change there has been is to
free speech, discussion of the Undiscussed.

One can doubt whether this is permanent. Let
the new King be a good king for a few years or so,
and it will again be the convention not to talk about
him too frankly. Not snobbery will see to that,
but the reticence and reverence that Majesty must
inspire.

This phase will soon be over. The unique thrill of
striking down the Idol will soon be repented and
forgotten—and all those curious currents which
there were, for that one shifting kaleidoscopic day or
two after the first shock. . . .

Then the ancient nation pulled itself together, saw
clear, with some remorse but no hesitation *slew* the

god who no longer "held good as the sacred taboo of the tribe's prosperity and propriety," and set up a new god in his Place.

The tribal Emblem in danger, the tribe did not desert it; but rallied around it more stoutly. It, not Him. Country and Empire were adamant to save It, and acted swiftly to that end only.

The theoretical issue they dismissed contemptuously. When, for the first time for hundreds of years, Republic versus Monarchy was put to the people's representatives, although the moment was monarchically unpropitious the Commons declared themselves by 403 votes to 5 against the Republic. Five votes out of four hundred and eight, or one eightieth, may be taken as fairly representing the proportion of republican sentiment in the country.

The personal issue was secondary, if painful to millions. There was deep regret, but on the majority side no real conflict of loyalties.

"The man is more interesting. The institution is more important. The monarchy matters more than the monarch."

A bit of a shock it had been, of course. Dummy had not played fair. Coming out like that as a human being. Developing tastes of his own that were not the tribe's; flouting mass prejudices.

Such a mishap, however, was felt as no general argument against kingship.

285

It happens so rarely. The last time was when James II—in Mass preference—flouted mass preference.

It can so easily be put right. It was.

All the rules were kept. By Dummy himself, after the one rule he broke that broke him. He hid in his Trianon, never once shewed himself to the crowd, and thus spared the Ministers awkwardness, or more. By Government and Opposition, conservatives and socialists, front bench and back bench, press and people.

At a turning which, in other lands, would have been the Revolution, the English character and the English calm, and the English way of doing things and of not doing things, asserted themselves, abundantly justified themselves. The Statute of Westminster worked. Baldwin worked it. The Empire held together. The Crown held it together; and it the Crown. Each Dominion could have seized the chance to declare itself a republic; but all of them, instantaneously, automatically, marvellously, acknowledged King George. Throughout Quarter-of-the-World not one single rule, or head, was broken. The car of the glorious British Constitution, without fuss, obstacle or upset, went forward in perfect order on its triumphal course.

If one poor small human being was crushed under the wheels, no matter.

It is no matter. To keep safe a way of government that is, for multitudes of men, a better way of government than the seen grisly alternatives—what matter if one man is sacrificed? Put it at its lowest. Some mumbo-jumbo a great people has to have: some emotional High Object. No milder or humaner, or politically more civilized, Object than the English Kingship could anyhow be found. So jealously keep it. Sacrifice ruthlessly anyone, even an English King, who endangers it.

We did.

Politically, therefore, this nation deserved all the congratulation, perhaps almost all the self-congratulation, that it received. The supplest system; the solidest nerves. Common sense and sense of proportion governing the day: good things which are the result, and cause, of a free constitution. No one except a few cads seeking to exploit the issue. Under a deluge of misrepresentation, a minimum of misunderstanding. False romantic quickly sorted from true. In a welter of excited inessentials, which old history and new journalism conspired to magnify, the essential—after the first shock, and those few hours' wavering—perceived, fastened upon and decisively made to prevail.

And yet: it was a perilous act, a perilous mean act. To dismiss so lightly a good and lawful king. To tamper, so easily, with mystery. After twenty-five years building a legend, in one savage week to destroy it; loosing the hounds to tear a beautiful god to pieces.

Even as politics is it pure gain? He was ignorant, superficial, they are now saying; quite unbalanced; a misfit, a morbid child. He messed up his private affairs, and would soon have messed up public affairs also. He liked stunts, flashy advice. Among politicians he liked the rogue elephants. He liked Lloyd George and Winston Churchill. It is comical, they say, to compare him to a great world statesman like Mr. Baldwin.

No one, of any school, aspires to. Only, while Edward (it is a flimsy, Fascist point) just *might* have got things done, Baldwin throughout Eternity quite certainly never will. If one of them had had his way instead of the other, there just might have been fewer people in Britain hungry and hopeless this winter and next.

That, however, is not Politics.

Morally, as distinct from politically, the self-congratulation has been a thought on the lavish side.

Not that the favourite foreign accusation, hypocrisy, seems justified more than usual. It was not hypocrisy, it was intellectual clarity (never a favourite foreign accusation), to refuse to mix up private and public emotions, as some did whose hearts were better than their heads; to shut eyes to purely private life, yet open them censoriously wide to exact a high standard of public living.

Nor should Rat Week bring odium upon the whole nation. After all, the friends of mistress and ex-Master who really distinguished themselves by the speed and depth of their Iscariotry hardly numbered more than a dozen. A high priestess of the revels, Lady (Simon) Peter found the neatest formula: "Of course, personally I *hardly* knew Her; now that it's all turned out so interesting, one almost *regrets* not having known her better . . ." Three times at one party, she repeated this; and immediately the cock crew. He crowed for a week without leaving off, in the Ritz Bar and other such places.

But in far wider circles than that, in the attitude of this country as a whole, there were aspects not admirable. There was slander about, as well as sense; baseness as well as beauty. More smut than even the circumstances called for; and a fair amount of deliberate cruel lying. Amid much English good nature, a deficiency of pity. For a quarter-century they had kissed his feet, and now they sacked him like a thieving servant—without even a month's notice. With no un-English self-doubting, a good average display of English self-content. If hypocrisy not above average, an excess of finnicking and fault-finding and miserable carping, and then, when all over , thick calm smooth oceans of complacency, Complacency, COMPLACENCY.

England, indeed, is very pleased with herself. She feels actually fitter than before. She has expelled from her system a foreign body which never really agreed with her: a piece of matter, come to think of it, damned odd for the House of Windsor ever to have produced and which, now she realizes, she was a bit anxious about all along. Probably anyway in the long run he would have———. It's far better really that it has happened. When all's said and done, we ought to be *thankful*. What I say is———

Enough, and much more, has been said.

Many other aspects therefore—the parts played by, cross-currents within, Dominions, Cabinet, Labour Party, Royal Family, Church, Press . . . the morganatic, mystic, financial, sexual, 'German,' 'American' aspects—of which some were not secondary and several are interesting, can safely be left to oblivion. Or to the future historian.

III

As history, it will be told by a much later time. As tragedy, by Second Shakespeare when he comes.

Who, in his fifth act, will treat the later life and the death of the Prince of Windsor.

Which may be triumphal, an answer serene or smashing (there are curious possibilities: how one would like to speak with him upon them) to his detractors; a great life doubling the great romance.

Which may be tragical. Or the worst chance, trivial.

He takes rank with the Great Lovers; his memory with Antony and Cleopatra, Tristram and Yseult, Paolo and Francesca, Romeo and Juliet. The sophisticated have no notion how powerful amongst poor and ignorant, and ordinary, people in every country Edward of England's romantic prestige has already become.

Women hold up their heads. After all, then, the girlhood dreams and the beautiful stories were *true*. Cynicism, sensuality, beastliness, self-interest were not the only things true. The chief of the kings of the earth cast away his crown for the sake of the woman he loved. Who might have been *me*.

No doubt, the two real living creatures are not equal to the high legendary parts they have created. The Man and assuredly the woman are less than the myth they have made.

As Myth they will abide. In this life, no one knows what will happen to them.

It is foreordained, anyway. As it all was fore-ordained.

On his stamps, back to the light and eyes looking into the shadows. Looking away from his Crown, behind him.

At his Father's funeral, the orb fell from the Crown.

The first King never to have King's weather. It drenched with rain when he went to open his only Parliament and at almost every other function of his eleven months.—He cut short this ceremony because of it, went on with that function despite it, and contrived (since he was vouchsafed little luck, and less generosity) to annoy a maximum number of people. Each single time the decision was taken out of unselfish consideration for others. But Society, which had insolence from a certain quarter to avenge, would see no good in anything he did; and turned thumbs down almost from the first hour.

December Eleventh, the same day that James II went; the last non-conformer and cashiered king.

A new dynasty on the throne, the eldest son has never in English history succeeded. Always it has been the Second Son.

"Kiss the Second Son!"

IV

That we are loyally and optimistically engaged in doing.

Everyone is trying to see the bright side. His Gracious Majesty Our Sovereign Lord KING GEORGE VI is trying to.

He fits in better. In the way most people want him to fit in. And all the important people.

The way they want now, at this perilous hour of the world.

England at last has become aware of her position, not at all what it was; of the shakiness of her ancient superiority; of frightful peril, near. This hour it is which welcomes the new love; which broke the old.

Bad luck, largely. *He* would have suited the nineteen-twenties; the bolder, looser, more carefree years. Lloyd George and All That. He did amazingly suit them. Sterner discipline now is needed: tradition, safe morality, the old virtues and values.

It is the same mood, for instance, not party-political at all, which—more than that Party's weak points and weaker leaders—keeps Labour out, despite its decenter programme. The same mood which now steels this lazy civilian people to the course it most hates, re-arming. The same mood which will defeat (for example) divorce reform; and Germany.

In easier times originality, anti-convention, non-conforming could be allowed the Symbol, as private amusement and ornament. But not just now.

Safety first: George the Sixth.

The ticklish question of the royal private life, which seems to crop up in about alternate reigns, has been laid safely and soberly to rest again. Once more we have had the luck to catch a man who, to help him bear the preposterous burden of his public life, needs no private life different from what it ought to be; who can conform easily to the rule that King must conform to his people's morality rather than his own, since in his case they are the same; who requires no distractions but conventional ones, no friends but English ones; who like his father is ordinary enough, amazing enough, to find it natural and sufficient all his life to know only the sort of people a Symbol King ought to know.

Like his father.

George VI has, as everybody knows, been put there deliberately to be George V second edition. (Georges Cinq *bis*.)

His masters are monotonously telling him so, almost too callously de-personalizing their new Servant. Even he is a human being, and may have surprises in store. They will be mild surprises, no doubt; agreeable ones.

Meantime, surely, surely, we have had our joyous fill of scandal and denigration? It is unseemly—and there is no reason to belittle this good and dutiful man. To suppose him dull, or stupid, or ignorant, or reactionary, or a bigot; or more conservative (small c or big) than the Head of a State, monarch or president, perforce must rightly be. To laugh at his former sobriquet "The Industrial Duke." He probably does not know very much about the organization, or the processes, or the working conditions of industry. But he knows more about these things than a majority of the gentlemen who lead the Conservative

Party; or than a majority of the gentlemen who lead the Labour Party.

Less brilliant, he brings Wife and Family to treble the Symbol's value. A gracious Queen. Those compensating little girls. A happy and decorous home life, emblematically ideal.

These are crushing advantages. One wonders, really, how we found the other adequate at all.

With one Exception, that compensating little girl is the most popular heir since the Middle Ages. The newspapers have spilt no sweat building *her* up. To her (from the Exception), with scarcely decent avidity and rapidity, sentiment is being wholesale transferred.

If I have a kink for a Queen, I share it with many men. Partly it is English history, partly spiritual-psychological. If not a woman, I would rather the Sovereign-Symbol was a celibate man. (Elizabeth, Edward.) For my taste a married king is too much like a married priest. That is a minority taste, evidently; but the other is general.

While in herself the small Princess-Presumptuous gives hope of a revival of great days, such as her great-great-grandmother saw to, and her great great namesake; and in her face looks more like tough Pride of England than any of the men.

Father is keeping her place warm.

George is victory against the foreigner; of homely tradition over exotic lack of tradition, safety over adventure, older generation—partly perhaps, though one doubts the theory—over younger. When the prestige, existence, of an old mighty empire are at stake, this is quite natural.

It is all quite natural. As guardian of moral conservatism, the National Government was a national government.

Political and social conservatism are less generally desired, and one of the new King's handicaps is that he is thought of as the man of the reactionaries. Quite unjustly. He came in as no party's nominee, but as a united political nation's.

He knows this himself. Lord Wigram knows it.

In any case he will have little influence on policy at first, and will sign merely, and on the dotted line. The Interlude is over. The influence he will later acquire will be mildly liberal, contrasting with a mildly conservative influence in the spheres of morals and manners; where as tribal god, he will mirror his people in their traditional soberer mood.

He will follow the new destiny, and be imperial; make no Adriatic and Levantine errings, but go forth to see and be seen of each State of the Empire he personifies.

He will move along the middle of the road, where England and Empire like him to be; the old road that leads through familiar places to continual destiny.

He will steady the throne, after the shake it has had. He will climb slowly, but surely, the steps to popularity; not arrive there at a bound as did the beloved (execrated) Exile. But he will arrive there, in time; and there stay.

Always supposing that he has been able to survive one curious danger:—a reaction in favour of the Dispossessed.

For one day, in nostalgy and boredom, a changed mood may come upon us. For these times, we shall then ask ourselves, *is* it only tradition and dull safety and careful sobriety that we need? Is not salvation through boldness, adventure, experiment, individuality, quick march in step with a newer world? What He stood for.

The Exile himself will not seek to profit. Only Balkan kings come back. Ourselves, we shall let the mood pass, and stick to the decision we rightly took and the man we rightly chose.

If there was jiggery-pokery, George of all men had no hand in it. We need this throne, and owe gratitude to the man who has accepted to sit on it; to this brave good ordinary man who, from sense of duty, with no desire of it, with no adequate sense of his fitness for it, with anxiety, prayer, modesty and self-sacrifice has in circumstances of private anguish and public difficulty taken over for us the

Headship of Imperial England, the most eminent and fantastic function in the world.

Even for an ordinary man the burden is extraordinary. King George needs and deserves more than our gratitude; he needs our help, and devotion; and a truce to chatter, miserable carping and ill-will.

He needs God's grace which soon now, in antique traditional setting of earthly splendour, will be vouchsafed him.

CORONATION

I

IN May he goes to be anointed, crowned and enthroned.

The Coronation is a rite.

For the Church of England one of her highest and strangest rites, resembling ordination, resembling consecration, resembling holy matrimony, by which she creates this unique *mixta persona*, half layman, half priest, and dedicates him to a lofty and unique relation to her and to the State; by which she blesses the political contract between him and his people, and through the Christian mystery makes it a sacramental contract between him and his God. For the older religion of England it is a maimed rite; celebrated in *their* ancient temple which they in love and the true faith built; a heretic sacrament administered by heretic hands. For the oldest religion of England it is a magical rite: they are turning a man into a god.

It is a political form.

A practical nation, the least unfree of the nations, deliberately and affectionately retains this archaic ritual as the supreme means of celebrating her unity, her continuity and her dominion. Government, deprived in all its other parts of mystery and beauty and stability—papers, printed forms, policemen, parliaments; a see-saw of factions, a constitution without checks—here stands forth for a moment as a thing of glory and permanence, an ancient sublime defiance of the mutability and materialism of other ages and of ours. From generation to generation the Lord's Anointed lives on. The richest man in the world cannot buy the humblest office at the ceremony. Millionaires cannot book seats in the Abbey—Mr. Pierpont Morgan, alone, crept into rich-man-loving Edward VII's crowning, as 'personal guest' of His Majesty—but trade unionists as of right are allotted them, and peers the most penniless. The practical foundations of the English State have wholly changed; its millennial mystical basis is seen to be unchangeable. Solitary in the world we have no National Day of patriotic commemoration. We have instead, and prefer, this fantastic occasional festival of England's sceptred duration and majestic transmission of England's sovereignty.

The *direct* political significance has, in certain obvious ways, declined. Formerly, when the kingship was still in some sort elective, it was a necessary confirmation by Church and people of the Witan's choice; now, when prince follows prince on the throne automatically, or almost automatically, it fulfils no such practical purpose. Of old, the Homage was important, shewing that the great

302

nobles gave the new king their essential support. In bygone days, when there were disputed successions, the king got himself consecrated as soon as he could—a matter of days after his accession—so as to dish all possible rivals:

Doth not the Crown of England prove the King?

Now that his title is undisputed and he becomes king by the bare fact of his predecessor's demise, now that he is monarch already without the oil and the diadem, his sacring can be put off, and is put off, even for a year or more.

Perhaps indeed too long. The modern reasons for postponement are, however, sound ones. Nowadays, as a rule, the dead (as a rule it is a dead) sovereign is popular, and his mourning must not be indecorously short. For a festival so general the slender chance of English good weather must be increased, so they wait till a May or June. With the complexity of modern life, long months of organization are needed. Since to-day he is king, not of a few counties in one little country but of many countries in every continent of the world, time must be allowed for the representatives of his remotest domains to make their plans, travel and come.

Imperially, the Coronation grows in importance each time. For George VI's, by the side of the older Court of Claims and the Coronation Committee of the Privy Council there was set up a Commission representative of the Dominions, "to consider those aspects of the arrangements for the Coronation which are of common concern to the Empire." So the supplest political system of history pursues its way, and brand-new nations at Antipodes take their rightful share in sacring the Saxon chief.

This time the solemnity will take on a certain practical significance again. There is no disputed succession, precisely, nor rivalry of title; but the oil and the diadem will add desirably to King George's strength. . . .

There is the juridical angle. This transmission of powers, some say, is legally necessary.

They are quite wrong. The Oath, the only part that law—the Act of Settlement—requires, does not require these ceremonies. Few of the world's few other remaining kings find it needful to be crowned. The Coronation is completely unnecessary.

So there is the aspect of Uniqueness. That ours is the exception, the insolent gorgeous anomaly, is a cause of pride. As in the glory, we rejoice in the singularity of it.

Yet for some, it is a matter of indifference. For those to whom all public affairs are indifferent; if not only those. Too much fuss over falderals: over a piece of play-acting that's taken a deal too seriously. So, one hundred years ago, thought Mr. Disraeli. He had no Court dress, and did not think it worth while to buy one. "I console myself," he said, "by the conviction that to get up very early—eight o'clock—to sit dressed like a flunkey in the Abbey for seven or eight hours, and to listen to a sermon by the Bishop of London, can be no great enjoyment." That hour was the zenith of rationalism (and *laissez faire*, and industrial cruelty), and the nadir of English monarchy. Dizzy was not yet a queen's darling: would he himself have said the same a generation later? Alike as ritual and spectacle, absolute low water mark was William IV's rather than Victoria's. After that one brief epoch of relative eclipse, Coronation has now re-acquired all its utmost prestige. Both at George IV's and William IV's the Abbey nave was in part empty; for George VI's you could fill it hundreds and thousands of times over. In 1937 the indifferents are immeasurably less numerous than in 1837.

For a few, however, it is a matter of more than in-difference. It is a farce, a foolery. A revue piece, over-advertised and over-exploited by every re-actionary interest. A barbaric puerile mummery. A raree-show that is a disgrace and a danger to the political intelligence of twentieth-century England; a costly and cold-hearted defiance of her poverty and problems. Cash will pour out, a river of millions, upon this Circus; and decline to a mean trickle for the needs of the hopeless and hungry.

For many, the busiest time of their lives. For Earl Marshal; for Great Chamberlain and High Con-stable, on this one day back in first place instead of

upstart Prime Minister and the Cabinet men. For
New Scotland Yard, for police and pickpockets,
detectives and crooks, traffic authorities and West
End trades, makers of flags and medals, makers of
mugs, exploiters of mugs . . .

There will be a greater gathering of people than
ever since the start of the world.

For the chief number—a spectacle and show. In a
world of drabness the best show left. A pageant more
splendid than any the dictators can put on: beating
Rome and Nuremberg hollow at their own bewilder-
ing best, and with no obverse side of compulsion or
horror. It is the desire of nations to see (not the
mystery in the Abbey, which is beyond sane hopes)
the great cortège: the King in his Glory.

Coronation after coronation, the cost of a first-
class seat on the route of the procession has risen, and
more than the value of money has declined:—from
a *blank* at the Conqueror's, a fuskin at John's, a
dodkin at Henry III's; a half-farthing at Edward I's,
a farthing at Edward II's, a half-penny at Edward III's,
a penny at Richard II's; half a groat at Henry VII's, a
whole groat at Henry VIII's, a tester at Queen
Elizabeth's . . . to ten guineas at George IV's,
twenty at George V's, and Heaven and the profiteers
know how many at George VI's. For the majority,
far from the capital, or with no such sums in their
pockets, the Coronation has put on equal strength
as an occasion of general rejoicing. Coronation Clubs

in the poorest parts assure decoration for the day, and something extra to eat and drink in its honour. Coronation Committees and schemes of the middle classes contrive memorials of the event that are more permanent, and perhaps as useful. Ox-roasting and dancing and beer; tree-planting and hospitals and parks. Amid the merriment, in the heart and mind of most, some dim notion of the historic meaning and millennial destiny.

For England, as nation among the nations—a glorious announcement of her chief place among them. From the four corners of the earth will come the principal persons from every people. About the central ceremony a round of pomps and shows: Courts, State banquets, Court balls; levees, investitures; Review of the Fleet, Trooping of the Colour; civic and imperial solemnities and junketings; parties for the rulers, popular rejoicings for the ruled; King's progress to Royal Scotland, princely Wales, the outer Empire—a great cycle of power and pageantry.

For the Man himself, the meaning in May will be—what? It would be irrelevant, irreverent, to try to guess.

One or two little changes have been made in the original arrangements.

Two persons will be crowned instead of one. The chief person will be a different person. Peeresses will wear coronets instead of tiaras.

Some think the addition of a queen adds interest. Others that the rite would have been more curious-mysterious with a lonely man alone. With *that* man, anyhow; whom they preferred, and say: The gilt is off the crown's gold.

But many feel that with the new King—more traditional, more impersonal, Symbol Pure—the rite gains.

Edward dreaded the day. George will have a friend by his side.

He will be reverent.

Above the Event, and the heads of most of us, specialists lovingly hover.

The *liturgiologist* lingers over one of the most interesting rituals in history; its most striking instance of an ancient ceremony that, through long ages of continual change, has scarcely changed. From the Pontifical of Egbert—from the Byzantine rites on which that was chiefly based—to the Form and Order for George VI, almost none of the essentials and not many of the details have varied. In the petty Saxon kingdom our world Empire is born from, the archbishop of the selfsame august and Augustine see upon the King's head poured oil, in his hand placed a sceptre and upon his head set a crown royal, the while our forefathers cried: May the King live for ever! The State has evolved from a tiny Teutonic chiefdom into a world-wide imperial

federation, its governing men from a Witenagemot
of Saxon tribesmen into a polled Parliament, from
feudal Assembly into the landowners' Parliament of
Victoria's coronation, the capitalists' Parliament of
Edward VII's, the ever more working-class Parliament of to-day; and through Conquest, Reformation,
Revolution and all the great transformations geograph-
ical, racial, confessional, political, industrial and social,
the King's Crowning has stayed the same.

Immutability so unparalleled has explanations.

It is a rite that in its fundamentals you cannot
change much. It is very rarely performed: forty
times or so these thousand years. We the English
have never much wanted to change it.

Wise adaptations to political fact and development
there have been; and changes of stress. Crown, in
place of Orb or Sceptre, has come to be considered
the chief token of regal power. The placing of it
upon the king's head has, instead of the divine
anointing, come to be considered—by the layman,
the majority—the principal part of the solemnity,
and as far back as the Middle Ages gave its name
to the whole series of ceremonies of which it is but
a part.

Details have dropped out. The Hereditary Herb-
women strew no longer their flowers before the
King's way. Dymoke the King's Champion no
longer—alas—in shining armour enters Westminster
Hall on horseback to throw down the gauntlet. The

Progress from the Tower is no more; though our new King, following the Uncrowned's desire, is unselfishly having the route of his procession extended: six and a half cheering tiring miles it will be. The Coronation Banquet is gone, and with it the Chief Butler, Chief Cupbearer, Chief Lardiner, Royal Napier, Grand Carver, Grand Pannetier, Lord of the Sewer, and all the rest of that glittering gastronomic crew. The essential, the rite and its essential meaning, stays the same.

The *regalianist* revels in thrones, sceptres, orbs; ampullas, bracelets, spurs, rings; robes, mantles, sandals, buskins; laurel-wreaths, diadems, mitres, talpaks, tiaras, crowns; their weight, worth, workmanship; their function and fame.

In celebrated crowns. Crown of Charlemagne; Crown of Saint Stephen; Iron Crown of Lombardy. The crown imperial that Lothair, forsaking king's palace for monk's cell, beat into a crucifix. The Crown of Wisdom, which is the Fear of the Lord. The crown of burning iron that John of Hungary set on the head of the rebel peasants' leader—

Were red-hot steel to sear me to the brain.

The crown that after Chæronea, Demosthenes dared not take; nor, after the Rubicon, Cæsar.

Their celebrated jewels. Orloff: Regent: Burning of Troy: Moon of Mountains. The Royal Ruby, or Garnet, for which Pedro the Cruel murdered the

Red King of Granada and then gave to the Black Prince his friend; and which still is England's. The Mountain of Light or *Koh-i-Noor*, once the peacock's eye in the Peacock Throne, with the possession of which goes the possession of India; and which still is England's.

The history of crowns from when, as in the ancient days, they were recompense for athletic or æsthetic prowess, for beautiful bodies and brilliant minds, in Hellas; for duty and courage—*corona muralis*, for the first soldier to scale the walls of a city, *corona civica*, *corona obsidionalis*, *corona triumphalis*—in Rome; for the priest, the bride, the martyr . . . until sovereignty's brows grew envious and gods and then kings appropriated them. Kings in the end will beat gods, who through the Middle Age still hold out. Jesus Christ still crowns His Mother; Holy Ghost crowns Mother and Son. Jesus offers Catherine a crown of diamonds and a crown of thorns; she chooses, seizes, kisses the thorns. The redeemed offer their crowns to the Redeemer. Kings theirs to the King of Kings.

How the kings of old time truly *wore* their crowns. William the Conqueror donned his many days each year, three times in high state: at Eastertide in Winchester, at Whitsuntide in Westminster, at Christmastide in Gloucester. Richard III wore his at Bosworth, Henry V his at Agincourt, Saul his at Mount Gilboa.

How they loved their crowns. Henry of Lancaster

liked his so well that he had it beside him on his very death-pillow:

Set me the crown upon the pillow here—

whence, he sleeping, Prince Harry his son stole it ambitiously to try on. Amazement of the World had seven crowns; of his seven kingdoms. At the end he bade them all be placed before him and, sadly gloating over them, died.

How revolutions defaced, destroyed, dispersed them; soiled them, spoiled them, sold them, stole them; put them in museums and mausoleums and their wearers in exile or on the block—until now, in the middle twentieth century, the only great historic diadem *in use* is England's. . . .

The *philosopher* views the yellow bauble with a more jaundiced eye. To wear it, men have trodden underfoot each law of heaven and earth; slain father and mother, and brother and sister, and friend; waded through seas of blood, trampled continents into deserts. It has been the brightest ambition, punished with the darkest penalties, of the horrible human race. With what high hopes they put it on, and in what low misery often lose it.

A crown
Golden in show, is but a wreath of thorns

At Montezuma's gorgeous crowning the King of Tezcuco, in that famous inauguration address, told the new emperor he would reign for many years, long and glorious. Then Cortes came.

They have small joy of it, most of them. Read Shakespeare. Read history. Read in their faces . . .

The philosopher, of course, is a little out of date. To-day a man is likelier to commit crime to evade a crown than to wear one. The thorns in the 1937 model are too spiky and painful altogether. We were only just able last December—after more times, it is said, than they tried with Cæsar; and because of his unusually deep and unselfish sense of duty—to *persuade* a man to wear ours.

Historian joins liturgist to compare this recension with that, to note and explain the points of likeness or of contrast between each succeeding celebration of the rite. In his own secular domain, he recovers political details, paltry and piquant details, and conjures up the whole social and constitutional setting of every recorded consecration from the first.

To others, not specialists—the laymen, the majority—chance of reading and caprice of memory shew a picture more broken. Dim childhood's recollection here; sudden light of drama or absurdity there; gaps for centuries. . . .

II

High Kings of Erin white-robed for their anointing on the Hill of Tara, or beneath the holy tree in the

Plain of Adoration at Adair. Lords of the Isles, giants, fixing their feet in the royal marks of the Stone of Islay. In a Britain of faery and springtime, Merlin amid the Giants' Dance at Stonehenge achieving with high sorcery of rites druidical the earthly apotheosis of King Arthur.

Saxon warriors enthroned on the King's Stone by Thames. Kings of Wessex, *Emperors of Albion*, hallowed in barbaric state (grey they seem, a pomp of shadows) in the old church of the old capital, Winchester; that London ousted from her place, as since childhood I have resented.

Egbert, first of the English authentic series, they crowned—across more than one thousand two hundred years they crowned—and Edward the Elder they crowned, with near the same ceremonies as awaited Edward the Younger.

Athelstan, my school-book told, was tossed high into the air by the loyalty and enthusiasm of his subjects.

Edwy the Fair got tired of the length of his coronation banquet, and preferring women to wine and his wife to other women, retired with her (whom the Church, most modernly, had just insulted by refusing to crown queen, because she was within their prohibited degrees) to a quiet room apart to enjoy her society to the full. The archbishop sent Dunstan to recall the King to table, and to a sense of his position. The priest, though appalled by what he saw—the Crown rolling about on the floor, and

not only the Crown—boldly separated them, dumped
the thing again on the king's unwilling head, and
dragged him back from pleasure to duty.

Ethelred the Unready also suffered from Dunstan
who, himself the archbishop now, turned his
coronation homily (most modernly) into a vicious
attack on the young king, accusing him of having
murdered Dunstan's little favourite, Edward the
Martyr; which was hard on Ethelred, who had just
been flogged with that big taper by Mamma for
disapproving of the murder.

1066 is the year of two coronations: the Conquered's, the Conqueror's. Before Saint Edward
was cold, the Last of the Saxons repaired to the dead
man's Abbey and on the morrow, Epiphany, which
was a very dark winter's afternoon, in gloom and
fear, in haste and confusion, got himself made the
King. Before the twelvemonth was quite gone, he
had been defeated and slain. On Christmas Day of
1066 his slayer, William the Bastard, stood the year's
second Anointed Man in the Abbey. It was a dark
winter's afternoon again. At the Recognition the
question had to be put twice, by the Norman prelate
in French to the conquerors, by the Saxon prelate in
English to the conquered. To hide their hate, and
fear, the company of the latter answered "Yea, yea:
King William!" with deliberate noise and zeal;
hearing which tumult, the Norman soldiers outside
thought it was rebellion, lost their heads and started

slaughtering the English around them and setting fire to the Abbey buildings. Inside, the flames lighted the darkness, and they heard the slaughter; in panic the great church emptied, and William with the priests was left standing alone by the altar. He trembled, as never before nor after; and the priests did. Both went on grimly to the end, through anointing, crowning, enthroning: until, with fullest traditional rites, the usurper had been made the lawful lord.

They anointed Stephen at the Feast of Stephen.

Henry II had three separate ceremonies: at Westminster, at Winchester, at Worcester.

Because of the hatred of them, it was thought humane to issue a proclamation forbidding Jews to come to Richard Lion-Heart's Coronation. But the aliens were curious to see and ambitious to be seen, and some of the leading usurers of London managed to get into the Banquet. The people spotted them, dragged them forth, murdered them, and started a horrible general slaughter of the Hebrews—'despatching their blood-suckers with blood to hell.'

John jeered. He declared himself so bored with it all that he left the Abbey before the end, without taking the Holy Sacrament; inaugurating with indignity his reign that ended in indignity and disaster. When, to invest him with the Duchy of Normandy, which still belonged to England, they placed the ritual spear in his hands, out of sheer evil insolence he threw it away. Five years later he threw

Normandy away. Likewise the Crown of England, that he mocked at as Hubert Walter placed it upon his head, a few years later he had basely to deliver to the papal legate; to receive back in contemptuous Petrine donation. At the end, crossing the Wash in flight from his subjects, he lost it in the waters.

As a little boy Henry III was crowned at Gloucester with his mother's bracelet. As a little boy I knew that. It is the first Coronation story we all knew.

Edward *I* being in Palestine when his father died, his coronation was put off for two years: an interval longer than our most modern ones. At Edward *II's* the dinner was bad, and Piers' practical arrangements worse. All was confusion, as the reign was. Magnificently dressed and bejewelled, Pierrot triumphed openly over the She-Wolf and took her place at the King's side. Edward *III*, trying to prove he was not privy to his mother's murder of his father, had engraved on his coronation medal a picture of a hand stretched out to catch a falling crown, with the words *Non rapit, sed recipit.* She-Wolf wept throughout the ceremony. Edward *IV*, because of the Roses and of bloody doubt as to who should wear it, only after two postponements managed to get the crown put on his head. For Edward *V* everything was ready, robes, regalia and all; but he got smothered first. In England's long list that poor boy is the only king uncrowned; except that poor boy Edward *VIII*, who got smothered first.

Henry VII, when Bosworth Field was won, found the crown all by itself in a thornbush; where Crookback, dying, and the Wars of the Roses and two generations of weak Lancastrian government had left it. Lord Stanley put it on the Welshman's head, there on a hill above the battle. With his slender title, Henry took care to get anointed and crowned in the Abbey as well; when he created, to protect his slender safety, the corps of the Yeoman of the Guard.

Bloody Mary would not occupy the Chair of State, soiled by her heretic little brother's body the time before. The oil too, through the Interdict, had lost its holiness: she must needs procure papally a fresh supply for her anointing.

Elizabeth's objection to the oil was as characteristic as her sister's, and less theological: merely that it stank. At that dividing hour between the two religions, she could get no archbishop and none of her sister's bishops, all Romans, to attend her consecration. No one of them would crown the bastard and heretic. At length, in borrowed robes, the old Bishop of Carlisle was bullied into officiating. Literally alone as modest representative of all the Church, he crowned her; and promptly died of remorse. To make up for the poverty of the religious ceremony, the Procession from the Tower and all the profane rejoicings were sumptuous in the extreme, as befitted the coming reign.

Like the close of it, the inauguration of the reign

318

of Charles the Martyr went all wrong. There could be no procession from the Tower, because of the Plague. The King's barge ran aground at Parliament stairs. The wing of the dove on the Confessor's sceptre got broken. The old Bishop of Carlisle (another one), who also died promptly (this time of ye black Jaundice), preached from the text "And I will give unto thee a crown of life"—not a life text but death text. There was an earthquake. The Queen refused to attend, to be Protestantly crowned. The Archbishop who anointed had hands tainted with killing a man. When he presented Charles to the people there followed—whether because they thought his speech was not finished, or because they could not hear what the old man said, or in horrible presage—instead of the usual acclamation a dead silence. In place of the traditional mantle of purple and gold, to declare the Virgin Purity with which on the Day of Purification he came to be espoused unto his Kingdom, our one Connoisseur King wore a robe of pure white: unlucky white, England's unlucky colour death-white. He looked, not a prince proceeding to his crowning, but what he was: a victim, White King and Dreadfull Dead-man, going to the sacrifice.

His murderer dared not be crowned, but as Lord Protector had himself enthroned in the Chair of Saint Edward, for that one and only time brought out of the Abbey and placed in Westminster Hall.

Charles II celebrated the return to kingship by

having a specially magnificent coronation. Old Juxon who crowned him had attended his father on the scaffold. The scene was affecting to both men. Charles's heart was not so cold as Macaulay made out.

Brother James, an honester stupider Papist, had the Communion Service omitted. Throughout the solemnity the Crown kept tumbling off his head; to fall off finally four short years later.

Little scarecrow William and big plump Mary were crowned together, joint sovereigns severally invested with the symbols of full sovereignty.

Queen Anne was so fat and gouty that in the standing-up parts of the ceremony she had to be *held* up. By traditional English bad manners to Queens' consorts, poor Prince George of Denmark was kept out of any share in the ceremony whatever. They let him come to the Banquet, however; and gave him plenty of beer.

Caroline drove up to the Abbey and at every door was turned away. "Your ticket?" they asked her. "I have none, and as Queen of England I need none." Sometimes above the cheering and the music within, the hostile shouts of the populace could be heard outside. George had queasy moments; wondering whether, despite all, she had managed to get in. Prince Esterhazy wore a glittering coat of jewels, worth £100,000, which cost him £200 to put on, as every time he was sure to lose pearls to that amount. For the last time King's Champion rode in, all armour, and threw down the gauntlet. Prinny's inauguration was the most gorgeous and most expensive of the modern age. His people called it a Punch-show, and his consecration a blasphemy, and the homage a kow-tow, and him a fat dressed-up old hog. Sir Walter Scott alone, one of the few likeable men who liked him, described it all with approval.

William IV tried to avoid being crowned altogether, but in the end the thing was done on the cheap: the Half-Crownation. Sailor Bill wore trousers, and the rite was tastelessly cut down. Young Victoria his heir did not attend, Hanoverian family rows being then at their height; the King insisting that she should follow instead of precede his royal brothers in the cortège up the Abbey, and the Duchess of Kent refusing to give way.

When Victoria's own turn came, stinginess was again the watchword: the Penny Crowning this time it was called. Royalty was so unpopular that it *dared* not have much money spent. The ceremony had been badly rehearsed; neither the clergy nor the Officers of the Household knew their parts. "Pray tell me what I am to do," asked the poor little queen, "for they" (all the big-bugs) "do not know." There was the affair of the too small ring, and of the orb too heavy for her to hold. Soult, the ex-enemy, was cheered more than Wellington his conqueror. The old marshal was quite overcome by this English generosity: "Ah, c'est un brave peuple!"

A sinister black *goose* was seen flying in the air that day; and so "She's not long for this world" was cheerfully foretold. "The last coronation England will see" was the day's more general prophecy.

Neither prophecy had fulfilment, for those famous sixty-four years later there came her son's.

I was walking back home from school, along Beech Grove. I had just crossed the road and set foot on the edge of the Stray, to cut across the grass to *Victoria* Avenue, when an errand boy, basket on arm, appeared suddenly as though from nowhere. "They've put t' Coronation off" he told me, "T' King's poorly," and then vanished; though on the open Stray there was nowhere, other than magically, he could have vanished to. Dazed by this apparition, this messenger for me alone, I stared in all directions. There was no errand boy, nobody, within sight anywhere. I ran home, and there learnt that my mysterious messenger's information was true.

For the postponed event they gave us tin mugs in Sunday School, with pictures on them of him and his Queen. The Mascots had a song:

> *On Coronation Day,*
> *On Coronation Day,*
> *We'll all be merry,*
> *Drinking whisky, wine and sherry:*
> *All be merry,*
> *On Coronation Day!*

George V came home to Windsor when, nine years after, his own enthronement was over. We bicycled over from another county to see. The Mayor and Corporation welcomed him at the Castle gates and he made a short speech in reply; standing all of them on a dais. Queen Mary looked taller than he did. It is the only time I ever saw him, or any other reigning sovereign of England. To my disappointment he was not wearing the Crown.

Beyond England:
Vague visions of Germanic chieftains and the *gyratio*. A horned warrior is upraised on a shield; he stands on it; upon the shoulders of the chief tribesmen he is borne round and round among the assembled people, the high Spear of Power held aloft in his hand, the people acclaiming. In a setting more gorgeous and purple, the Prætorians elevate their chosen Imperator of Eternal Rome upon the *scudo*. Amid clamour of Greens and Blues in the Hippodrome, wan Byzantine emperors and fiendish empresses-regnant mount the throne:

Mighty and prosperous and august, prosperously, prosperously.

Many years thou shalt reign. God will keep this realm, God will keep this Christian realm. Abundance to the world! As thou hast lived, so rule. Incorrupt rulers for the world! Kyrie eleison.

Worthy of the Empire: worthy of the Trinity: worthy

323

of the City! Piously hast thou lived, piously reign. Thou
conquerest! God hath given you, God will keep you.

Mighty and prosperous and august, prosperously,
prosperously . . .

Sardanapalus assumes the diadem by direct order
of Astarte, Queen of Love. Pharaoh is crowned with
a double diadem: the Red Crown of the Delta, above
it the White Crown of the South. There are carried
three thousand crowns of pure gold in the coronation
pomps of his heirs, the Ptolemies; whose last heir,
clad in the white name and linen of Isis, mounts silver
steps to a high throne of gold, Mark Antony her lover
in purple and diamonds at her side. The pale Inca
is crowned incestuously with the Ccoya, his wife-
sister; he wears the crown with the two radiant wing
feathers of the coraquenque. The dark Negus (now
also, even since I write, no more), King of Kings,
Lion of Judah, calls to the virgins who challenge him
and bar his way, "I am the King of Zion"; with
his sabre cuts the crimson cord they have drawn
before the church of crowning, and triumphally goes
in. Tsar Nicholas I, his face 'hard as Siberian ice,'
moves to the Kremlin amid subjects dropped on their
faces in the dust, not daring to cheer, or even look . .
Dim differential scenes of pomp and glory in Babylon,
Nineveh, Persepolis, Ispahan; Rheims, Aix-la-
Chapelle, Milan, Pressburg, Toledo; Rio, Bangkok,
Pekin.

The trees went forth on a time to anoint a King over them.

Before the Successor of the Fisherman the Ceremonarius lights the flax. It flares a brief moment, and goes out. *Pater Sancte, sic transit gloria mundi.*

A thousand years before Christ's birth, in Christ's country, there was a man called Saul. A choice young man, and a goodly; there was not among the children of Israel a goodlier person than he; from his shoulders and upward he was higher than any of the people. When Samuel saw Saul, the Lord said unto him: "Behold the man whom I spoke to thee of! This same shall reign over my people." Then Samuel took a vial of oil, and poured it upon his head, and kissed him. And the Spirit of the Lord came upon him, and he was turned into another man: God gave him another heart. And Samuel said to all the people: "See ye him whom the Lord hath chosen." And the people shouted, and said: "God save the King!" And so King David—"Arise, anoint him: for this is he!" —and so more ritually King Solomon, and King Jehoida, and other princes of Jewry. Upon the head of Vashti, upon the head of Esther her supplantress, Ahasuerus-Artaxerxes sets the crown royal.

Clovis the heathen conqueror of Gaul was baptized, confirmed, crowned in the same night: Christmas Eve of 496. St. Remi led the savage warrior to the font: "Humble thyself, Sicambrian! Burn what thou hast worshipped, and worship that which thou hast burnt!" Clovis said his belief in the Holy Trinity, was dipped in the holy laver, then anointed as first of the long glorious line of Most Christian Kings. In Rheims again, near a thousand years later, Charles VII stood with the crown upon his head. The Maid who had won it for him stood by his side. Then she knelt down before the king she had made, and kissed his feet and covered them with warm tears; she who had delivered for him the very fair country of France from the English, to whom she was soon to be delivered for burning.

Christmas Night of eight hundred, in old St. Peter's, the Pope had been artful and clapped the crown quick on Charlemagne's head. Eighteen hundred and four, in Notre-Dame, the second Charlemagne was artfuller and placed brazenly the golden laurel-wreath upon his own Corsican brow: the half-captive pontiff a mere looker-on, the Church this time clear second. She had been first so often. As when Adrian IV refused to sacre mighty Barbarossa until the Kaiser humbly held his stirrup, helped him down from his horse, stood like a base menial beside him: him, Nicholas Breakspear of Langley, Hertford-shire; him, Vicar of Christ.

In a little land in the north, poor and violent, a baby girl but nine months old wailed in fear as rough men took her from her cradle and as the Earl of Arran held her in his arms and the Cardinal Beaufort forced her tiny fingers for an instant round the sceptre and as they held the great Crown a moment on her head and feigned girding her with the great Sword of State. She wept all through, as her poor father in "infectious passion" of tears had wept before her, as she herself afterwards was to weep; the turbulent lords in superstitious presage noted it. Regnant of Scotland, Consort of France, Claimant of England, through the most romantic life any woman ever has lived she met also tragedy, and did great crime; loved much, and is forgiven. . . .

Beyond crownings, decrownings.

As when in Kenilworth Castle they took unhappy Edward II, and stripped him of his honours and every kingly ornament, and put him in plain black. The Archbishop—again—preached a face-saving, time-serving sermon on *Vox populi, vox Dei;* text most unarchiepiscopal. The three estates renounced their homage. The Lord Steward broke his staff, as when a king dies. The heralds proclaimed degradingly "Sir Edward, *late* King of England . . ." [1]

Self-decrownings: compulsory, as when Henry of Lancaster forced Richard of Bordeaux

> *With his own tears to wash away his balm,*
> *With his own hands to give away the crown,*
> *With his own tongue decry his sacred state;*

[1] Compare unhappy Edward VIII. Prince Edward, *late* King of England.

or voluntary, of which several strange instances are remembered.

Diocletian, dramatically divesting himself of the purple in the wide plain of Nicomedia. Emperor Justin of Byzantium removing the diadem from his own brow; placing it on the head of the successor he had chosen, Tiberius the Beautiful, who humbly knelt; making the most famous of all King's Speeches: "You are receiving the ensigns of power not from my hand, but from the hand of God. I have been dazzled by the splendour of the diadem: be thou wise and modest. I have sinned; those who have inflamed my passions will appear with me before the tribunal of Christ. Delight not in blood. Love your people like yourself. . . ." Charles V; Philip V. King Gustavus Vasa: King-Queen Christine.

She signed her deed of resignation. She rose from a silver throne. Amid a silence and great sadness she delivered the orb and the sceptre. She took off her crown; disrobed herself of her royal mantle; stood before them in a dress of plain white taffeta. She made a moving speech on the past and future of Sweden. She walked slowly out.

Beyond all the great queens and kings of this world: The Man whom they ritually stripped, on whom they put a robe of scarlet, and a sceptre (a reed) into his right hand; for whom they plaited a crown (of thorns) and put it on his head; before whom they bowed the knee, upon whom they spat, and whom they mocked crying: HAIL KING OF THE JEWS!

The chief priests likewise mocked, saying: He saved others, himself he cannot save.

Pilate saith unto them: Behold the Man.

III

This was the King of Kings. His subject, the King of England, now goes to be crowned.

With his wife the Queen he will set forth from his Palace in cavalcade through cheering hosts, the largest in history, for the Abbey of Westminster; there alighting to take his place, chief place in it and the world, in the golden mediæval procession that will enter the Abbey.

As he goes in by the great West Door, and his eyes see within the minster, crowded with people, ablaze with colour, beautiful, and all eyes seek him, voices will greet him as they greeted his forefathers singing the ancient psalm: *I was glad when they said unto me, We will go into the house of the Lord.*

Processionally eastward King and Queen will pass up the church, the body and choir of the church, into the high *Theatre* or Mount of the mystery.

They will pass their thrones, make their humble

adoration, and kneel down at their faldstools in private prayer.

. . . .

The rite begins.

The metropolitan of England by thousand-year-old precedent makes PRESENTATION of him to the People.

Preceded by Garter King of Arms and accompanied fourfold, by the Lord High Chancellor of England, the Lord Great Chamberlain of England, the Lord High Constable of England, the Earl Marshal of England, the Archbishop goes to each of the four sides of the Mount, first the east, then the south, then the west, then the north side and—while the King stands and turns and shews himself to the four points of heaven—speaks with a loud voice, saying: *Sirs, I here present unto you King GEORGE, the undoubted King of this Realm: Wherefore all you who are come this day to do your homage and service, Are you willing to do the same?*

Not rarely this has been no mere rhetorical, ritual question. There has been doubt, and fear, what the multitude's answer would be. The Conqueror feared and doubted. Archbishop Hubert Walter required the throng's acclamation before he would take upon himself the anointing of a man like John. As late as George I some uncertainty attended the response. The Jacobites stood around with sullen faces:

"But," said my Lady Dorchester to Lady Cowper, "when there are so many drawn swords, does the old fool really think that anybody will say *No?*"

In May, although through few minds and hearts a certain thought will not be passing, real doubt or fear of the answer there will hardly be. In answer to the Archbishop's question all the people in the Abbey, led by the Westminster schoolboys, will signify their willingness and joy by loud and repeated acclamations, with one voice crying out:

God save King GEORGE.

And the trumpets will sound.

This, the RECOGNITION by the People, preserves the pre-historic tradition that the king is chosen by them, the chief by his tribesmen; the millennary tradition that the Witan is submitting its candidate for the nation to approve, and that the king, if indicated by heredity, is made by tumultuary choice.

A religious, Christian part follows this vestige of the pagan-political: Litany, Communion, Epistle, Gospel (Render unto Cæsar . . .), Creed, Sermon.

The Archbishop administers the OATH.

He goes to the King and asks him: *Sir, is Your Majesty willing to take the Oath?* And the King answering, *I am willing*—

Will you solemnly promise and swear to govern the Peoples of Great Britain, Ireland, Canada, Australia, New Zealand and the Union of South Africa, of your Possessions and the other Territories to any of them belonging or pertaining, and of your Empire of India, according to their respective laws or customs?

I solemnly promise so to do.

Will you to your power cause Law and Justice, in Mercy, to be executed in all your judgements?

I will.

Will you to the utmost of your power maintain the Laws of God, and the true Profession of the Gospel? Will you to the utmost of your power maintain in the United Kingdom the Protestant Reformed Religion established by law? And will you maintain and preserve inviolably the Settlement of the Church of England, and the Doctrine, Worship, Discipline, and Government thereof, as by law established in England? And will you preserve unto the Bishops and Clergy of England, and to the Churches there committed to their charge, all such rights and privileges as by law do or shall appertain to them, or any of them?

All this I promise to do.

The King then arises out of his chair and, the Sword of State being carried before him, goes to the Altar and, uncovered, makes his solemn Oath in the sight of all the people; laying his right hand upon the Holy Gospel (open at St. John) in the Great Bible, and saying these words:

*The things which I have herebefore promised, I will
perform, and keep.*

So help me God.

He will kiss the Book and sign the Oath—our King
contractually.

The *Veni, Creator Spiritus,* the Archbishop's sacring
prayer, the chanting of *Zadok the priest* . . . and,
having been disrobed of his crimson robe by the Lord
Great Chamberlain, and his white breast made bare,
the King will sit down in the Chair of Saint Edward
for the high moment of his HALLOWING or
ANOINTING.

Four Knights of the Garter will hold up over him
the Pall of Cloth of Gold, and the Archbishop will
take the Holy Oil and with it will reverently anoint
him in the form of a cross:

On the crown of the head, saying,

*Be thy Head anointed with the holy Oil, as kings,
priests, and prophets were anointed.*

On the breast, saying,

Be thy Breast anointed with holy Oil.

On the palm of both the hands, saying,

Be thy Hands anointed with holy Oil.

*And as Solomon was anointed king by Zadok the priest
and Nathan the prophet, so be you anointed, blessed, and
consecrated King over this People, whom the Lord your God*

*hath given you to rule and govern, In the Name of the
Father, and of the Son, and of the Holy Ghost. Amen.*

On head, breast, hands: for knowledge, valour,
glory.

Sacring instant is the most sacred instant. By
unction, grace is conferred upon the office, and the
sevenfold gift of the Holy Ghost upon its holder. The
Spirit of the Lord comes upon him, and he is turned
into another man.

It is the high instant of life for the kings themselves;
from which few have not gained ghostly strength,
and which has left its lasting mark, for their own
souls' and their people's good, upon many. At the
mystical minute, two only of all the long line
of England shewed indifference: the worst, John,
who giggled and jeered: the best, Elizabeth, who
sniffed and complained, "This grease smelleth ill."

Now he is the Lord's Anointed; like anachronistic
King Lear, a man of 'anointed flesh.'

> *Not all the waters in the rough rude sea*
> *Can wash the balm from an anointed king.*

Half priest, half man, *rex idemque sacerdos*, they
deck him in the sacerdotal vestments. With the
Colombium Sindonis, or Saint Edward's tunic. With
Saint Edward's mantle, or the Supertunica, or Close
Pall of Cloth of Gold.

Then, blended of religious elements and knightly

elements, of military, historical and political elements, there follows the INVESTITURE with the insignia of chivalry and of royalty.

They touch his heels with the Golden Spurs; gird him with the kingly Sword of Justice—*With this Sword do justice, stop the growth of iniquity, protect the Holy Church of God, help and defend widows and orphans, restore the things that are gone to decay, maintain the things that are restored, punish and reform what is amiss, and confirm what is in good order*—and clothe him with the dalmatic, or imperial mantle, or Robe Royal of purple silk.

They place in his hand the Orb with the Cross, the Archbishop saying to him: *When you see this Orb thus set under the Cross, remember that the whole world is subject to the Power and Empire of Christ our Redeemer.*

The Orb he delivers again to be laid by the Dean of Westminster on the Altar; having, though a sacrèd man and royal, only two hands like the rest of us—and the two Sceptres still to be held in them.

The Archbishop puts upon the King's finger the Ring, the Wedding Ring of England.

By this he is consecrated to her: a Queen Regnant to *him*. From time forgotten the giving of a ring has signified imparting of authority: as of Pharaoh to Joseph, Ahasuerus to Mordecai, Tiberius to Caligula, his father to the Prodigal Son. The closer the Ring of England fits the king's finger, the longer will be his reign and the better beloved will he be. Victoria proved it once again. The ring by mistake had been made to fit her little finger, but rightly and ritually the Archbishop insisted on putting it on the fourth, the marrying finger. It hurt her abominably (she could get it off afterwards only by holding her hand for some time in iced water), but she made no sound of complaint, no more than at any other physical pain or danger during her reign of sixty-four years; which was, as prophesied, the pain's reward. When to that predecessor of Victoria's she so strangely hated, subjects had come humbly to urge matrimony, Gloriana held up her hand, shewed them the ring, and answered: "Look, I am wedded already. England is my husband."

The Lord of the Manor of Worksop presents the Glove.

They deliver to him the Sceptre Royal with the Cross, set with the Star of Africa, the largest diamond of the world, ensign of kingly power and justice; and the Rod with the Dove, emblem of kingly equity and mercy, consecrating him to the service of the State, to rule it firmly but with lovingkindness.

The CROWNING moment.

The Archbishop, having prayed—*O God, the Crown of the faithful: Bless we beseech thee and sanctify this thy servant GEORGE our King: and as thou dost this day set a Crown of pure Gold upon his Head, so enrich his Royal Heart with thine abundant grace, and crown him with all princely virtues, through the King Eternal Jesus Christ our Lord*—then will take the Crown of *SAINT EDWARD* and reverently put it upon the head of *KING GEORGE*.

At the mysterious tremendous sight whereof the people, with loud, joyful and repeated shouts, will cry—as they cried for King Saul three thousand years ago in Jewry, when Priam still was King of Troy—

GOD SAVE THE KING,

the while the Peers and the Kings of Arms will put on their coronets; and the trumpets will sound and, outside, the joyful bells; and, by a signal given, timed to the instant of crowning, the great guns at the Tower will be fired off.

The Archbishop will pray, *God crown you with a crown of glory and righteousness*.

The choir will sing, *Be strong and play the man: Keep the commandments of the Lord thy God, and walk in His ways*.

They will present him with the Holy Bible. He will receive the Benediction. He will be ready for his INTHRONIZATION.

Into his high throne they will lift him, as of old his pagan ancestors were lifted upon the shield, while all the prelates and Great Officers and great nobles stand around.

The Archbishop will face him, and say: *Establish*

your Throne in righteousness, that it may stand fast for evermore.

All will come in their order to do him HOMAGE on his throne.

The Archbishop will kneel down before His Majesty's knees, and say his homage and kiss him. *Kiss the Son.* Then the bishops; then the Princes of the Blood. Then dukes, marquesses, earls, viscounts, barons; the senior of each rank singly ascending the throne, stretching forth his hand, touching the Crown on His Majesty's head, and saying: *I do become your Liege man of Life and Limb, and of earthly worship; and faith and truth I will bear unto you, to live and die, against all manner of folks. So help me God.*

When the great ones' Homage is ended, the drums will beat and the trumpets sound, and all the PEOPLE in the Abbey will shout, crying out:

> *God save King GEORGE*
> *Long live King GEORGE*
> *May the King live for ever.*

The most antique mystery known; and will be telegraphed, broadcast, filmed.

They will crown his QUEEN.

He will kneel down; offer Bread and Wine. The Exhortation, Confession, Absolution.

338

He will eat the body; drink the blood. The Post-Communion, Gloria in Excelsis, Te Deum Laudamus.

And then, in his right hand the Sceptre with the Cross and in his left the Orb, crowned and robed in all his magnificence, power and glory he will go forth to his people and his fate.

THE END